Emotional
FITNESS

FROM CHALLENGE TO CHAMPION
IN 60 DAYS

DOUGLAS
WEISS, PH.D.

Emotional Fitness
© 2015 1st Edition
by Douglas Weiss, Ph.D.

Requests for information:
Discovery Press
heart2heart@xc.org
719-278-3708

Interior and Cover design by: Janelle Evangelides
Edited by: Christianwriterhelp.com
Printed in the United States of America

CONTENTS

Introduction

One universal, dynamic malady affects many of us, regardless of where we live on this vast planet we call Earth. Though this malady inflicts untold damage upon our lives and the lives of those we love, it often goes undetected.

I am not talking about global warming, war, or political corruption. No, I am talking about something more personal: an epidemic lack of emotional fitness. To put it another way: emotional cluelessness.

A man sitting in my office, headed toward divorce but seeking a miracle to save his marriage, admitted with wisdom and humility, "I wouldn't know a feeling if it hit me in the face." His sentiment expresses a universal problem, a problem I have encountered in the men, women, and teens I have counseled over the last twenty years.

However, I encounter the lack of emotional intelligence not only in my practice, but also in my own life. Like the man just mentioned, at one time, I couldn't recognize my feelings. I came from a family like many of the families my readers grew up in; we never talked about feelings except in an extreme or dysfunctional manner. Like many others, this emotional cluelessness left me unequipped and unprepared for life. As a result, as a teen and young adult, I walked straight into multiple addictions and dysfunctional relationships.

Though I had a spiritual awakening at nineteen, I still remained emotionally unfit through college and even into adulthood. As a future counselor, I knew I would need to understand my emotions, because only then could I counsel others toward understanding their own. Motivated, I looked into option after option in an effort to learn about my feelings, only to come to the conclusion that no class, teacher, or book could teach me what I wanted and needed to learn. I was totally dysfunctional and totally unable to identify or communicate my feelings. I was, quite literally, emotionally out of shape and in need of a trainer, but no trainer could I find.

Then and there, I decided I would need to serve as my own trainer, my own teacher. I created tools to help me start to manage my emotions. Over time, I found success, moving from a novice to an emotional black belt. I started to understand my feelings, and in turn, myself. The best part was, my newfound abilities (which I will teach you about in the following pages), impacted every aspect of my life, from my marriage to my business to my relationship with my God.

Given their impact on my life, I realized the tools I had created for my personal use could impact others. They were transferable and could be used to teach others how to move into an emotionally fit lifestyle!

I am not going to tell you such a move does not take work. It takes a lot of work—hard work—but by doing the work, you can change from emotionally unfit to emotionally fit, and it will benefit all aspects of your life. Now, are you ready to get fit?

What Is Emotional Fitness?

This is a journey. Though perhaps unfamiliar to you, it is a road that has been traveled by many, many I have come into contact with both through my clinical practice and through speaking at conferences.

I live in Colorado, and part of living here is daily seeing a visual symbol of the unfamiliar journey: Pike's Peak, the beautiful behemoth, rising in my view whenever I look west. It's a mountain for the hiker to conquer—or at least attempt to conquer. Every successful trip, though, starts at the bottom of the trail and moves upward, one step at a time. So let's start this journey together, not up Pike's Peak, but to another kind of summit: emotional fitness.-

Once you reach the summit, you will have an emotional fitness that allows you to see the world as it truly is: a spectacular place. Congratulations for your willingness to begin this journey, a journey that requires courage.

Before we start this journey, you will need to know what to bring with you. Every traveler must be prepared.

Right now, we are at the base of the mountain and reaching the top seems daunting, but for those willing to work, impossibility is merely an illusion. With the right attitude and the right preparation, seekers can reach the summit of emotional fitness and even have fun while doing it.

You might be tempted to fixate on how out of shape you are or how lacking in resolve. Or, you may be eager for the hike. Whether you are sure you can do this or not, relax and focus. Get ready to pace yourself. You can and will make it!

Skills

"Dr. Weiss, if all of us have feelings, then why can't most of us do this emotional stuff?" Carol, a forty-two-year-old, highly successful executive and mother of three asked me, sitting in a small group of her peers. Her question is one I have heard so many times I have lost count.

So let me digress for just a moment and draw an analogy. Let's talk about diets. Typically when you think about dieting, you think about your carbs, proteins, sugars, calories, and fats. You think about your metabolism and regimen of physical exercise.

There was once a day, generations ago, when people did not think at all about the healthiness of what they ate. They ate whatever and whenever they wanted, without a thought to any kind of consequence for their behavior. People in those generations often died young due to the lack of information and skills that would have helped them determine the appropriate diet for an optimally healthy life.

Just as our Western culture entered an era of awareness of diet and physical fitness, our culture is about to enter a new awareness of the role of emotional fitness, how it affects human life, human relationships, and even physical health.

Being emotionally fit is a skill to be acquired but it can only be acquired after the reality of feelings and emotional fitness is presented. Typically, when someone wants to talk about their feelings, we might be intrigued but easily become confused.

The feeling evoked is almost like the one we experience watching Olympic gymnasts competing. We are amazed at how the athletes move. However, then something in our thinking changes and fear enters in. We ask ourselves, *How is it that the athletes jump around with no apparent fear of getting hurt? or How do they look confident as they go through routines that are so obviously dangerous?*

An athlete's safety net is skills developed through practice, through drills. I have known many athletes, especially in Colorado Springs where the Olympic Training Center is located, and they all rely on skills to become some of the world's elite.

Like a gymnast's skills, emotional fitness must be developed. And this development often comes through the observation of a mentor, someone who has developed emotional skills. Often, frustratingly, most of us have not known someone emotionally fit.

Think about your own life for a moment. Let's start early: junior high. Think about the emotions you had at that time and your experience of others articulating emotions to you. Most remember expressions of anger but not much else beyond that. In many cases, the same is true for your high school and college experiences: almost no expression of any emotion except anger or a scant few other feelings. Therefore, most of us grew up emotionally impoverished.

Learning skills is the first key in understanding emotional fitness. However, skills alone do not produce world-class champions.

Work

This is where the rubber meets the road. Those who hope to accomplish their goals are different from those who actually do accomplish their goals. Those who accomplish their goals actually do the work to achieve their success.

Now that I'm over fifty, I periodically gain weight. Most of you are familiar with the problematic habits of eating late, making poor eating choices, and avoiding exercise—all of which lead to weight gain.

These problematic habits caused my weight gains, anywhere from a few pounds to as many as twenty. When I realized my weight gain, I was faced with a decision: Do I keep my newly gained weight, or do I decide to lose it?

It will do me no good to desire to lose the weight unless I implement changes in my behavior, setting goals that are realistic and attainable and use my willpower to change my behavior to reach these goals.

When I choose to change my behavior to lose weight, I lose it successfully every time.

Let's go back to our gymnasts. Olympians choose to forgo much of their social lives just as they forgo making large amounts of money and submit themselves to grueling daily workouts so they can achieve excellence. Because they choose hard work, they are successful.

Work is the single divider between those who master a new skill and those who don't. As an example, let me present to you my son, Jubal. When Jubal was five years old, he was introduced to the world of martial arts. During practices, he was given the skills necessary for a black belt in the making. At each belt testing, Jubal was given a choice: continue to work toward the black belt or give up.

Along the way he was challenged to quit numerous times, but he never did as the desire to obtain the black belt overshadowed any other desire. In the end, he passed his test and earned his black belt. On that day, his smile simply lit up a room. His hard work led him to a worthwhile goal. Likewise, emotional fitness, also a worthwhile goal, takes work.

Once people understand this process is going to require hard work, they are more ready to start the important journey to become emotionally fit.

Process

Commitment to the process is important to success in any enterprise. Many of us who went to college had at least one highly demanding college professor. We submitted to the professor's demands, not because we didn't have anything better to do, but because we realized that our professor was leading us toward a goal—and an important one. We needed to do the hard work of writing papers and preparing for tests in order to achieve this important goal: graduation.

For any momentous goal, there is a process that usually involves multiple steps, as in the case of emotional fitness. The goal of emotional fitness is also one that will require working through a multistep process. Unlike me, who had no guide, however, you will have a mentor, a guide. You will get to benefit from my experience and from that of those brave clients of mine who have worked through the process of emotional fitness. Along the way, I promise to expose you to the skills I have acquired on my journey and outline the work I have done that you will need to do. Because I have pioneered the trail, your journey will not be as long and tiresome as mine was, and in the end, your efforts will pay off with amazing lifelong results. Even better, your destination of emotional fitness will be uniquely yours.

The only thing I ask of you is a promise to commit to the journey. Let me guide you as you read this book, completing the tasks I set before you, doing the work I give you.

I have walked this trail with many before you and I have watched how their lives have transformed. Join me. This journey was mine, and now it is yours!

What Is an Emotion?

What is a feeling? Now that's the million-dollar question. When was the last time you really tried to define what a feeling or an emotion actually is?

Is an emotion purely a chemical process that happens to you? If you have ever experienced a feeling, you know it is way more than just a chemical process in your brain. So how can we define what an emotion is?

For our purposes, we will define a feeling or emotion as a momentary experience that may be tangibly expressed in an intricate manner by the entire being. What do I mean by expressing feelings throughout your entire being? As you journey with me, I assure you that if you do the work of emotional fitness, you will not only be able to connect with that definition, you will have lived that definition repeatedly through the pages ahead of you.

Emotions are extremely complicated to perceive and then utilize effectively. For example, think of your body. You can locate your body's parts and distinguish one part from another. In contrast, emotions do not appear to exist in predetermined locations. You might feel fear in one location or you might feel it throughout your entire body. You might feel calm in the region of your heart, but you might feel it throughout your entire spirit, soul, and body. Sadly, there is not a map of buttons on your body that will create feelings or identify feelings.

How do feelings travel? Do they travel just through the brain, the muscles, or the nerves? There is no conclusive evidence establishing how emotions travel throughout the body.

The purpose of emotions has some perceptional qualities. Take a walk in the forest in the dark and just as your senses are heightened, your feelings are heightened. Using a more common example, during even just an ordinary day at work you emote, sense, and feel your environment just as you do in your relationships with people.

Perception can easily be a purpose of emotions. Responding to environmental stimuli or to relationships is definitely a function of your emotions. You all have had the experience of walking by someone in a public area and feeling their acceptance of you. Their emotions are responding to their environment even though they may never have spoken about or thought much about their response.

Your emotions can respond to threats in your environment. You can respond emotionally if you feel someone is angry or upset at you. Try not to respond when your child does something amazing. Your emotions will just well up within you, again, without much thought.

Perception and response are functions or purposes of emotions. Influence and change are also functions. Your emotions impact, influence, and change an environment.

Have you been in an environment when someone became very angry? Their anger was felt and experienced by everyone, often eliciting alarm, fear, fight, and even flight. This chain reaction of emotion is going off throughout people in the environment.

What about the movies you watch? They want you to attach to the characters and can evoke all kinds of emotions. I remember watching the faith-based movie *Courageous*. The entire theater full of men cried tears of pride in response to the movie.

Emotions can change an environment as well. Think of this as a function that few really understand and master except great actors and actresses. Take being around someone who just insists on staying positive, loving, or excited. In time, their raw emotions can change the environment.

One evening, I was watching my son Jubal play in his high school football game. Jubal played both defensive and offensive line. In this game, his team was down and performing poorly. Suddenly, I saw him on the field, expressing some really strong emotions towards the players on the sideline telling them to encourage his teammates on the field. In the stands, we thought he was talking to us to cheer louder. Instantly, the bleachers started to cheer more. His intense emotion changed the environment.

As you work through your journey of emotional fitness, you will be able to change environments and relationships by choosing how you want to feel and how intensely you want to express any given feeling.

Now that we have a working understanding of what an emotion is and its purpose, I am going to switch topics and discuss what feelings are not. When speaking with clients of all ages, genders, beliefs and backgrounds, I am absolutely amazed at what people believe feelings and emotions really are. Some well-meaning therapists have told my clients some real whoppers as to what feelings are. In light of these experiences, I want to spend a few moments on what feelings are not.

Feelings are not facts. I know this may come as a surprise to some, but feelings are definitely not facts. The fact may be that you are having a feeling, but your feeling is not a fact.

Here is the problem: Feelings are genuine, but through some internal processes you can have misinterpretation before, during, or after your experience of that feeling. You can assume meaning where no meaning can be found in the rational world.

One day, I was lying in bed next to my wife, and I was feeling unsuccessful. The facts were that I had just been on a major television show, my book sales were doing well, and my marriage was in a really good spot. Feeling unsuccessful was not a fact; it was a feeling.

I am not saying feelings or emotions have no value. They absolutely do. However, they are not facts. Unlike numbers, they can be manipulated or even bubble up for no known reason. I can't tell you how many women I have met who feel ugly when the facts did not support their emotions. I have also met men who feel confident when facts did not support their confidence. Feelings and emotions are not facts.

Understanding this point is critical. If you think or truly believe your emotions are facts, you can take yourself and those around you on some pretty crazy and bizarre rides. You will stubbornly believe that because you feel something, it is based on fact, while your friends, spouse, children, or coworkers try to help you see a fact that is different than how you feel.

Feeling a feeling is just that, a momentary event that in no way indicates a fact is within a hundred miles of your experience. As you move forward in your emotional fitness, you will be able to see that feelings are just feelings. Then you will also have less need to strongly interpret them. The more you lose your hold on a meaning or interpretation of an emotion, the healthier you will be for yourself and those around you.

Feelings are not truth. Some people go beyond the belief that their feelings are facts to a belief that their feelings are expressions of truth. For me, truth is external, never changing, while by definition, feelings are temporal and ever changing. Just today, you have probably had many different feelings. Some of you had different feelings about the same event or person as you collected more information or saw the situation through a wider lens.

When a person believes feelings are truth, he or she is set up to be regularly misunderstood, avoided, and can become demanding, controlling, and easily offended by anyone who doesn't agree with his or her emotional reality.

Over the years, I have occasionally experienced something similar in my office. Most of my counseling is with sexual addicts. One wife found us on the Internet because she absolutely felt her husband was cheating on her—she would bet her life on it. She wanted me to break him down and have him confess so they could move on. He stated that over the course of their marriage he had never even kissed another woman. She emotionally knew the truth even though his stated reality was different.

Luckily, I have access to a polygraph examiner in my office. The couple agreed to have him perform the polygraph under the condition that the result of the polygraph is truth, regardless of what either emotionally believes.

He took the polygraph and passed it. The polygraph proved he had never cheated on his wife or even kissed another woman while married to her. His wife had to accept that her emotions were not truth. (I have had many other cases where the wife's feelings were spot-on regarding her husband's infidelity.)

The danger zone happens when you see your emotions as truth, especially the absolute truth; you are on a dangerous path to insanity.

Emotions are just emotions. As you walk through the following chapters, you will learn to separate emotions and learn to feel them fully, but not make them truth or facts. After all, they are simply emotions.

Your emotions need to be identified and processed for you to be emotionally healthy. As you move away from the perception that feelings are expressions of fact or truth, you will be more capable of having the ability to identify and process your emotions, leading you to emotional fitness.

Feelings are not needs. I have had clients improperly taught that their feelings are needs. The next thing they are taught is that their spouse or others are to meet these needs.

Let me clarify what a need really is. This is not meant to sound brash, but I want to be clear. A need is not a want, desire, wish, or luxury. A need is not something you need in order to be comfortable. A need is something you need to stay alive; without it you would die.

You and I *need* air, water, food, and shelter. If you have a medical condition or are in an accident in which you require medical attention to live, you have a need. Often people who buy in to the idea that emotions are needs enslave those around them to meet their needs for almost anything, and come to resent others when it doesn't happen.

A husband who says he needs affection would do better to say he desires affection. A woman who tells her husband she needs him to put the toilet seat down would do better to say she prefers that he put the toilet seat down.

When one person uses the word "need" repeatedly, it's not truthful and often causes others to feel manipulated and avoid the person, if possible. This person purchased an idea of "I feel, so I need, so someone else must meet my need."

They are close to the right idea. They do feel and, again, emotions are just emotions. An emotion can help you discover a lack in your immediate life. However, once you find a lack in your life, it is your responsibility to fill that lack and meet that need.

In scenario one, suppose Jack is feeling stressed and realizes he would feel better if he exercised. He goes to his wife, Traci, and tells her he needs her to go for a walk with him, or that she needs to go on a bike ride with him, or that she needs to go to the gym with him. Traci might ask why, to which Jack might reply, "I feel stressed and you need to exercise with me."

Scenario two is a better way for Jack to deal with his situation. In it, he tells his wife he is stressed and that, after helping the kids with homework, he is going on a thirty-minute run. Jack has identified his need, taken responsibility for what he lacks, followed through by communicating what he will do, and then actually did it.

In the first scenario, Traci would feel helpless as Jack makes his feelings her responsibility. In the second scenario, Traci would experience what it is to be married to an emotionally adult person who can identify his feelings, communicate them, take responsibility for them, make a plan, and follow through.

When we believe feelings are needs, we make life harder for ourselves and those around us. However, a feeling may lead you to a legitimate lack. When we take responsibility to address our emotional directives, we are more emotionally fit adults.

I believe it was important to provide you with this concise explanation about what feelings are and what they are not before you step on the path to emotional fitness. My hope is your journey will be amazing as you experience feelings in your entire being.

Emotional Fitness

Think back. Are you able to remember where you were when you first learned about your emotions? By the time you read the first sentence of this book, you had experienced millions of feelings over your lifetime. Now, where were you the first time you were actually taught about your emotions?

I want to share an experience about, not emotions, but thinking. I remember exactly where I was when I really began to think. I had had experiences of having thoughts many times prior to it, but I never really learned to think.

It was an ordinary day in my senior year of high school. Up until then, I had taken many tests, memorized many facts, but never really put any thought into it. I can remember walking into my classroom and sitting down at my desk.

That day we had a substitute teacher who said he was a philosophy student at a local college. He started class by telling us that he wasn't there to teach us a class but to teach us to think. He started to talk about a chair, just a regular chair, and all the different ways to think about a chair.

At that moment, something started to awaken inside of me. I was actually getting the abstract concepts he was expressing. I began to think, learn, get outside the box, and actually experience and communicate my own thoughts. This type of thinking has continued from that moment many years ago until now. Even my family comments that I never stop thinking.

That moment changed my life, my relationships, my health, and drove me into further education and into becoming a nonstop student of the human soul. Now, really think about this question: Where were you when you learned to feel your emotions?

Were you at home? In my family of origin, we never discussed feelings. Like many families, our feelings came out in three ways: angry, really angry, and I do not know. Hopefully your family was a little better, but my experience as a counselor shows me that many people received very little training about their emotions in their families of origin.

How about school? Did they teach you how to identify or communicate your emotions? Maybe you had the privilege of seeing a skilled counselor at school, but otherwise you were on your own as your emotions were developing through childhood, adolescence, and adulthood.

Think about your spiritual, athletic, and political communities. Sadly, each group developed a different part of your being, so they may not have been a place to really get an emotional education.

What about your friends? Growing up, my friends were as unskilled about feelings as I was. We could talk about school, teachers, each other, the game, but I don't ever remember sharing a feeling with a friend.

Most of us cannot really pinpoint a time when we actually learned how to feel or communicate our emotions appropriately. Our culture and our surroundings were telling us that emotions are unimportant.

Human beings have moved on for thousands of years with very little formal training in one of our very core aspects as human beings. In the chapters ahead, I intend to change that and prepare everyone who is willing to keep reading and do the emotional fitness work to become emotionally fit.

Imagine if when you were asked how you felt, you could intelligently communicate your exact feeling in that moment? Emotional fitness is much like physical fitness. We all have a body, but how many of us can actually say we are physically fit?

Physically fit people have different habits or disciplines than those who are not. First, a physically fit people value physical fitness. Second, they are committed to their value as demonstrated by a measurable set of behaviors. Third, a physically fit person is a result of these activities. They feel more confident, sharper, and more alive than a person who is not physically fit.

The same is true for an emotionally fit person. This person values emotions and is committed to some regimen focused toward getting and staying fit. Like the physically fit person, the emotionally fit person feels more aware, more confident, and more clear about himself and those around him.

This is not the time to worry about how emotionally unfit you may be. If you keep reading this book and do the work ahead, the changes you experience will amaze you. Think about all the weight loss ads you have seen in the past, the ones that depict the before and after pictures of people who are using their products. Unfortunately, I cannot show you the same physical results of becoming emotionally fit. However, as you become more fit, you will start to notice the blank, dull, disconnectedness in those who are not fit.

I have experienced the contrast between the before and after countless times in my office. After a few sessions, I watch the brightness coming into people's eyes as they are equipped to become emotionally fit.

Recently, some former clients came back into my office since they were back in town for a conference. Before I go into the results of their emotional fitness, I want to give you some background information on Luke and Laurie.

Luke and Laurie are not Americans, and in their culture, feelings are really ignored. After being married for years and having no children, they came to me to address their intimacy anorexia, which is defined as a withholding of intimacy toward a spouse. They both struggled with withholding intimacy emotionally, spiritually, and physically. During their sessions, I had them run through the emotional fitness exercises in this book.

When Luke and Laurie came back into my office, I was surprised at how bright their eyes were, how alive and authentic they appeared, and how much in love they were with each other.

I have watched countless journeys of individuals and couples coming into emotional fitness. The people who take this journey are significantly different, and I will elaborate on that in an upcoming chapter. I want you to see how emotional fitness is similar to physical fitness. It's available for all who are willing to take the journey.

As you will recall, I live in Colorado. One of the many hobbies those living in Colorado enjoy is hiking. We hike trails, parks, and even mountains. Those who choose to climb mountains say it is the most exhilarating experience of their lives. But it all starts with one step.

At the beginning, the trail seems relatively easy. The trees and grass surround you, comforting you like an old friend. As you keep going, you realize how the trail has become increasingly harder, offering you more of a challenge and making you exert more effort to get to the peak. You then realize how the trees and grass are no longer around you, because you have passed the tree line, where now you have only tundra to look at. Many people might think, *If even trees cannot grow here, then what I am doing here?* Coloradoans avoid that logic and simply consider the peak is just that much closer. By now, muscles are working harder, lungs are trying to breathe thinner air, but you keep pushing forward because you are so close. Failure to continue is not an option. You literally take one step at a time, stop periodically to rest and drink but ultimately keep going.

Then "it" happens. You place your foot on the peak. Celebrating, you begin to look all around. The view of the valley or city below is astounding. You did it! You congratulate yourself and face the reality of going down.

Becoming emotionally fit is kind of like hiking. In the beginning, it is a fun journey. Along the way, as you master emotions, you actually feel some emotions for the first time. Some feelings are more challenging for you, and as you push through, your mastery of emotions begins to accelerate. You learn new things about yourself and others as you continue. Emotional fitness is a lifestyle change so you can experience living every day. It allows you to taste life more fully and more richly than you ever dreamed you could.

The good news about emotional fitness is, it does not matter what age you are. I had the amazing experience of watching a couple in their eighties become more alive, more able to enjoy each other than they had when they became emotionally fit.

My personal journey to emotional fitness might break any preconceived notions you might have about Dr. Doug. Many people have heard me speak at conferences and think, *I bet he was raised in a really good family. He's probably never been through anything really hard. He's just lucky, healthy, blessed.* There seems to be this preconceived notion that my past positive circumstances have given me the tools I needed to live life and thrive in present relationships. I want to encourage you that after you hear my journey, I hope you can conclude that if I can do it, so can you. There is hope for you to take charge of your emotional fitness and do whatever is necessary to have a better life and to become more real and authentic in all your relationships.

My story starts before I was born. My mom was married, but had an affair which resulted in her being pregnant with me. Her husband divorced her and the man who got her pregnant supposedly had another woman pregnant at the same time, and abandoned my mother for the other woman.

That left my mom divorced and very pregnant. She did what she thought was best and went to a bar. There she reconnected with a man she already knew. His name was Weiss, and he married my pregnant mom, thus becoming my legal father.

After being married for a few years and two more children later, my mom could not put up with his alcoholism and behaviors that go with being married to an alcoholic. There she was, divorced for the second time, with three children and pregnant with the fourth. She realized she could not afford to support us and did what she thought was best, put us in foster care.

All I remember about foster care was being in a home for a while and then being taken to another home for a while. Eventually, before I started first grade, my mom met another man in a bar and they started living together. This man was not an alcoholic, and they were able to get the three of us out of foster care (the baby she was carrying was put up for adoption). As we progressed through grade school, my legal father would pay us occasional visits, though he had psychiatric issues and was often hospitalized.

When I reached junior high school, my mom decided it was time for me to receive my sex education. Neither my mom nor my stepdad had graduated from high school, so we had no books in our home. I was surprised when she walked into my room with a college textbook on sexuality. I do not remember reading much of this book, but the pictures were helpful in establishing what would become a full-blown sexual addiction.

Some time later, while walking across town, I was picked up by a man. He got me extremely drunk and sexually abused me. That started me on a path toward pornography and regular sexual encounters with older women. This is when alcohol and drugs came into my life like a landslide. During high school, I was drunk or high regularly, barely able to graduate.

At nineteen, I had a spiritual awakening, and soon alcohol and drugs were no longer part of my life. The sex addiction stuck though. That August, I enrolled in Bible college. I grew spiritually, but emotionally I was a clueless, constipated, self-medicating mess.

I met a wonderful Christian girl and fell in love with her; we married after my first year in seminary. That is when I started to clean up my sexual addiction. Shortly after marriage, I became free from sexual addiction and have been clean for more than 28 years.

I also changed my degree from Divinity to both Divinity and Marriage and Family Counseling. It was in a counseling class that I had an experience much like the one I had in high school with the substitute teacher. I sat in the back row and from that vantage point, observed the professor beginning to lecture. He was, sadly, unable to hold my attention. As I tried to keep my eyes open, I started looking through one of the books for the class. Contained in it was a list of feelings.

Suddenly, a realization hit me. I knew the professor was going to teach me about the importance of feelings, but not teach me how to feel. This was a profound awakening to a very stark reality. I was training myself to be a therapist, but I did not know a feeling if it hit me in the face. I had feelings, but I was about as emotionally illiterate as a twenty-four-year-old could be. This left me in a panic. If my professors are not going to teach me, then who was?

I received a crystal clear answer after I came down from my panic. I was going to have to teach myself. No books, teachers, or preachers were going to be able to help me. I remembered the list of feelings I had looked at earlier that day and realized I could teach myself to identify feelings. I knew that if I could learn the alphabet, a little French, Hebrew, and Greek, then I could learn feelings.

I developed an exercise for myself and solicited the help of the most beautiful woman in my life, Lisa. With her, we would identify and communicate feelings every day. We still do this, now twenty-five years later to keep ourselves emotionally fit.

I had to address the difficult feelings of abandonment, rejection, and anger that come when a soul is subjected to the circumstances to which I had been subjected. I had to be willing to aggressively let myself fully feel the pain I had either suppressed or medicated away in the past. These exercises helped me feel and process the pain I felt from the past. They helped me keep from running and shutting my emotional fitness down.

I have worked hard to get emotionally fit, and at times have had to work hard again, but I am worth being emotionally fit. My wife and children are worth having an emotionally fit husband and father. So are my friends, clients, and others in my life.

Your emotional illiteracy does not have to limit you one bit. I have become an emotional black belt. I now not only know what I am feeling, but I can usually sense the feelings of others. I am a man, a real man. I work out. I work hard. I love to compete. I have guy friends, and yes, I can share feelings. Gender is not a limitation. If you are a man reading this book, the possible benefits for you are tremendous.

Emotional fitness is a result of a known set of disciplines. This takes all the mystery out of becoming emotionally fit. It also robs you of any excuse not to become and stay emotionally fit. Just like getting in shape physically, emotional fitness starts with a decision, continues with a discipline, and ends in a result.

I had that moment almost thirty years ago. I had to be brutally honest to admit I was truly emotionally illiterate. Then, I had to take full responsibility to teach myself to become emotionally fit. I tell my clients, "it is good news if you are the problem. That means you are the solution." I say the same to you. Regardless of your past history, present circumstances, gender, or current emotional literacy, you can absolutely become emotionally fit.

From Clutter to Clean

Carol and Jake have been married for twenty-five years and have three children, two of whom are teenagers. This family has a typical evening pattern. Jake comes home from work, kisses his wife, and tries to talk with his daughter, who can usually be found parked on the living room sofa.

She is typically listening to her phone, disconnected from the family. Jake motions for her to take her ear buds out and asks gently, "How was your day?"

In typically teenage manner, she answers in short, one-word sentences like, "Fine."

Jake starts again, "Anything go on today?"

Again, "No," as she sits looking at her dad impatiently.

"Any homework?"

"Of course," she says with a glare as she hops off the sofa and storms off to her room, slamming the door.

~

Jennifer is a bank executive. She has worked at the same bank for many years, starting as a teller and later being promoted to an executive position. She has always been known to work extra hours and dresses extremely professionally. Jennifer just returned from maternity leave. After a few weeks, her boss notices that her reports are not getting done on time and some are missing significant information. When he confronts her about this lapse, Jennifer starts to cry. Unable to speak, she sits in his office a few minutes, then stands up and excuses herself and walks out of the office.

~

Tom has worked in the same office with the same schedule for more than twenty years. He has the reputation of being competent and generally effective at what he does. Every day, when Tom gets home from work, he and his wife, Maggie, discuss their day over dinner. As Tom walks through his interactions, Maggie asks him, "So, how did you feel?"

Almost startled by the question, Tom looks at Maggie and chooses to continue on with his story. Again, she stops him and asks, "How did you feel?"

This time Tom is frustrated and responds, "I didn't feel. I was just talking..."

~

These stories have something in common. Each person in the story had no idea what he or she felt. Many of us know the feeling of drawing a blank when someone asks us what we are feeling.

We were born with an almost infinite amount of emotion, but most of us never learned the skill of identifying specific feelings. Emotions were difficult for me because of my family of origin. As I have said before, I knew of only angry, really angry, and I do not know.

Angry was telling someone that something they did "ticked me off." Really angry included cursing, yelling, and slamming doors. "I don't know" or "I don't care" meant I did not have a clue how I felt, so I would leave the house and go for a walk or drive.

Your family may have been different. You may have been allowed to express your feelings. One woman told me that in her family, they were only allowed to express two feelings: fine or happy. In her family, happiness was expected, so she was always expected to be fine. That is tough. Especially when life throws you curve balls and challenging relationships and you are expected to be fine.

You have your own experiences and rules in your family of origin. Before we go any further, I want you to write in below what you experienced in your family regarding the sharing of feelings.

_____

_____

_____

_____

_____

_____

_____

Now that you have identified experiences growing up, I want to see if you can identify with some family rules regarding sharing emotions. The following are some rules that I have heard most frequently from clients regarding their families' thoughts about emotions.

Never have a feeling: In this family, you were not allowed to have any feelings, good or bad. Feelings were not communicated; actually they were discouraged. To survive in this family, you basically had to ignore all of your emotional self.

Feeling resulted in shaming: In this family, you were ridiculed for actually having a feeling. If you risked fear, pain, or even happiness, you chose to be the brunt of jokes.

Feelings indicated weakness: Many men and some women grew up with this rule. In this family, any emotional expressions were seen as indications of weakness. Instead of being shamed or joked about, you were pitied.

Happy feelings are okay: In this family you could feel upbeat, but if you did not, you were told to go to your room or outside to get over your negativity. Feelings other than positive ones were thought to be a private thing and something you were to get over like you would a cold.

Feelings are fine: Some people grew up able to express their feelings in healthy ways. In their families, feelings were not threatening and were often talked about and honored.

Below, I want you to write out a few of the rules I have mentioned with which you identify. See if you can share more about them or if other rules existed in your family or with your caretakers.

1. _____

_____

2. _____

_____

3. _____

_____

4. _____

_____

Beyond Your Past

As I have shared about my family, and possibly your family, you may have realized that all families have their strengths and weaknesses. I know I learned a great work ethic from my family. On the negative side, I did not learn to value education, to feel, or to save money.

You may have weaknesses that you learned from your family. That we can outgrow any weakness we have learned in our family is a wonderful truth. I have watched women who had less than satisfactory mothers become great mothers. I have seen men whose dads were drunks and broke all the time go on to become wealthy and sober.

Regardless of your past, you can get informed, make better choices, and choose friends and communities that will help you grow.

In the next few pages, we are going to start training to make you emotionally fit. Through these exercises, you will be able to know what you are feeling, communicate what you feel, and even change how you feel. If you are a parent, you will be able to model emotional fitness for your children. They can experience emotional fitness early on and live out the benefits of your hard work.

At first, you might not feel your children will benefit from your efforts, but that is the blessing of being a parent. You get to pass on to your children who you are and what you have. I have seen the amazing results of emotional fitness in many families, and it is a sight to behold!

First Things First

Think about your first day in first grade or kindergarten. I had a beautiful first grade teacher, Mrs. Most. She was kind, patient, and prone to giving a daily hug. She was amazing. Mrs. Most did not start us off on sentence structures, nouns, or pronouns in first grade. Had she done that, we would have been confused and failed the class. Like many first graders at that time, I did not even know how to read or write. So Mrs. Most started us with learning the alphabet. The alphabet is the first thing children learn in any culture with a written language. It provides the building blocks of language.

To learn a language you have to start with the basics. Even though you are a competent adult, emotional literacy starts with the basics as well. I call this the beginning stage of emotional fitness: feeling identification.

I am not going to ask you to abstractly find a feeling, as that might feel like mission impossible. To put things into perspective, I want to give you an illustration I have used for the last two decades. We all have hundreds of feelings, but for most of us it feels like the proverbial messy desk.

Though your desk is a mess, everything you need is there. You would argue that you can find anything there, given the time. Feelings work the same way: we have them, but they are not organized, and it may take us a while to find them.

The exercise I am going to share with you is one I designed for myself in an attempt to make myself more emotionally literate and emotionally fit. I felt hopeless and overwhelmed when I started this process. I did not have a clue, a mentor, or a direction; still, I knew I needed to start somewhere if I was going to get better at identifying feelings.

This exercise was inspired by an idea derived from the early computers. My roommate had a new computer with a primitive word processor. If you were typing a paper and you wanted to save your work, you had to have a least two characters in this file. You also had to put a label on your file, so the computer would be able to separate this paper from previous papers. To find your paper, you would type the file name and wait because it would take forever to open your paper. The efficiency of doing papers this way, rather than using a typewriter, saved us much needed time. I will show you how to create an emotional file inside yourself that will also help you to find your emotions much more efficiently.

Emotion Identification

It is time to start moving from cluttered to clean. Let's start separating your sticky notes from your envelopes and actually see what your desk looks like. You are about to start compiling your emotional alphabet.

Some of you may be tempted to skip over this part. This exercise may seem remedial, especially if you can skillfully communicate a handful of emotions. Emotional fitness allows you to take your range skillfully, intelligently, effortlessly, and efficiently into the one to two hundred range. When I speak at a conference and have a person randomly pick a feeling off a list of feelings and do it effortlessly, I know I am in peak emotional fitness. You can have that same skill and ease, even under pressure, but you have to start with the basic work to be able to progress to an amazingly emotionally fit lifestyle.

Below is a list of six emotions that are usually easy to work with. I am confident you will be able to do what I am asking you to do when identifying these feelings.

Calm	**Frustrated**	**Bold**
Amused	**Creative**	**Eager**

The first part of emotion identification is learning to identify the emotion in the present. Below, write out when you feel each of these emotions. I will give you an example, after which, you should identify how you experience this emotion.

Calm: I feel calm when I am in the hammock on my back porch, when no one else is home and I have nothing to do.

Calm: I feel calm when _____

_____

_____

Bold: I feel bold when my wife asks me to deal with someone on the phone who is not respecting her because she is a woman.

Bold: I feel bold when_____

_____

_____

Creative: I feel creative when someone asks me for business or marketing advice.

Creative: I feel creative when_____

_____

_____

Frustrated: I feel frustrated when the airlines keep changing my departure time because I have to make a connection in order to arrive at a conference.

Frustrated: I feel frustrated when_____

_____

_____

Amused: I feel amused when my teenage children are acting silly.

Amused: I feel amused when_____

_____

_____

Eager: I feel eager to get to the gym when I haven't worked out for a few days.

Eager: I feel eager when _____

_____

_____

Congratulations. You are now starting to identify your feelings. By taking the time to fill in the above statements, you show you are able to successfully go inside and find those feelings.

Remember the analogy I used about early computers needing two characters to save a file. I find this is true with emotions as well. If you actually had a second file on the same emotions, you are more likely to locate that emotion permanently.

I meet many new people regularly, whether I travel or remain in my office. Each person I meet has a name, and it is respectful to address each person by name. I used to struggle with remembering names until someone shared with me a tip for keeping the person's name in my memory. They told me to say the person's name three times in speaking to them the first time I met them.

I am going to use this example to illustrate the next part of the emotion identification exercise. With this tip, you will have a much greater chance of retaining the emotional tag when you need it. Your brain will easily locate and open that file for you in the future.

In the next part of this exercise, I want you to go as far back as you can to remember the first time you felt a particular feeling. Make it a point to go as far back as before the age of eighteen for all your examples. These two emotions do not have to be connected to the same experience. An example of connecting the two emotional statements may look like this: "I feel excited when I open a Christmas present. I first remember feeling excited when I opened a Christmas present when I was eight years old."

Oftentimes the first time we felt something can be radically different than the present. For example, you may feel excited when a family member is coming to visit. The first time you felt excited was when you won a sporting event in elementary school.

Give yourself time to explore these older sticky notes on the desk of your mind. You record many of life's events emotionally and cognitively. It may seem challenging at first, but do not give up. Once you start exercising your emotions, you will be amazed at how much you are able to access your emotions as you work through the second part of the emotions identification exercise.

I have used the same feeling words we worked with before. With each word, I am going to give an example of the first time I remember feeling that feeling. Then you write your first memory of that feeling. Remember, the example should have occurred before you turned eighteen.

Calm: I first remember feeling calm when my sister and I were at a farm together, lying on a grassy hill, making shapes out of the clouds. I was about nine.

Calm: I first remember feeling calm when _____

_____

_____

Bold: I first remember feeling bold when I was about fourteen, and I saw a big kid picking on a much smaller kid. I had my mom stop the car and I ran across the street and got in the bigger kid's face until he backed down.

Bold: I first remember feeling bold when_____

_____

_____

Creative: I first remember feeling creative in junior high when we were making masks using papier-mache.

Creative: I first remember feeling creative when _____

_____

_____

Frustrated: I first remember feeling frustrated when I was trying to put back together a radio I took apart when I was about six.

Frustrated: I first remember feeling frustrated when _____

_____

_____

Amused: I first remember feeling amused at a state fair my parents took me to in elementary school.

Amused: I first remember feeling amused when _____

_____

_____

Eager: I first remember feeling eager to play with my first dog, Cesar, when I was in first grade.

Eager: I first remember feeling eager when _____

_____

_____

Great job! You have successfully completed identifying six emotions. The emotions identification is part of your foundation for emotional fitness.

To successfully complete feelings identification, simply write out a feeling word.

For example, write "daring."

Then complete the following two statements:

I feel daring when _____

_____

_____

I first remember feeling daring when _____

_____

_____

My recommendation is to do this exercise using at least three emotions a day—three emotions of your choice. You will find a list of emotions in the Appendix. Simply pick one, do the exercise using it, and then pick another. I do not recommend that you go down the list, starting with the letter A. Instead, randomly pick emotions from the list or create another system that works for you.

Regardless of how you choose to approach the emotion identification exercise, it is really important that you practice this exercise regularly, and eventually work through the entire list. If you find some emotions challenging, do not avoid them. Just do the best you can with them. You might consider marking the more challenging feelings so you can come back to them as you progress through this book.

I am your emotions coach. You might feel emotionally out of shape, but if you actually do the work I am suggesting, refuse to cheat yourself, and remain consistent, you are going to look and feel emotionally amazing. On the next page is a worksheet to help you keep track of how many emotions you identified each day for the next ninety days.

Day 1 ____	Day 31 ____	Day 61 ____
Day 2 ____	Day 32 ____	Day 62 ____
Day 3 ____	Day 33 ____	Day 63 ____
Day 4 ____	Day 34 ____	Day 64 ____
Day 5 ____	Day 35 ____	Day 65 ____
Day 6 ____	Day 36 ____	Day 66 ____
Day 7 ____	Day 37 ____	Day 67 ____
Day 8 ____	Day 38 ____	Day 68 ____
Day 9 ____	Day 39 ____	Day 69 ____
Day 10 ____	Day 40 ____	Day 70 ____
Day 11 ____	Day 41 ____	Day 71 ____
Day 12 ____	Day 42 ____	Day 72 ____
Day 13 ____	Day 43 ____	Day 73 ____
Day 14 ____	Day 44 ____	Day 74 ____
Day 15 ____	Day 45 ____	Day 75 ____
Day 16 ____	Day 46 ____	Day 76 ____
Day 17 ____	Day 47 ____	Day 77 ____
Day 18 ____	Day 48 ____	Day 78 ____
Day 19 ____	Day 49 ____	Day 79 ____
Day 20 ____	Day 50 ____	Day 80 ____
Day 21 ____	Day 51 ____	Day 81 ____
Day 22 ____	Day 52 ____	Day 82 ____
Day 23 ____	Day 53 ____	Day 83 ____
Day 24 ____	Day 54 ____	Day 84 ____
Day 25 ____	Day 55 ____	Day 85 ____
Day 26 ____	Day 56 ____	Day 86 ____
Day 27 ____	Day 57 ____	Day 87 ____
Day 28 ____	Day 58 ____	Day 88 ____
Day 29 ____	Day 59 ____	Day 89 ____
Day 30 ____	Day 60 ____	Day 90 ____

Communicating Emotions

One of the most miraculous days of my life happened almost twenty years ago: the birth of my beautiful baby girl, Hadassah. Over time, Hadassah went from oohing, aahing, and crying, to saying "Dada" and "Mama," to saying short words and simple sentences. As she grew older, we started teaching Hadassah her letters. We would read to her and over time, her communication skills developed to such a degree that in high school, she competed in the state debate championships.

Just as Hadassah went through a process to learn how to communicate her first words, you and I will go through a process as we move from where we are in our emotional literacy to emotional fitness.

Congratulations, you have moved beyond your first step—identifying emotions—and are ready to take your second step. If you had a chance between chapters to write out some of your feelings, it will make this chapter easier for you.

In learning to speak and read fluently, Hadassah had to do much more than identify letters and words in books. If you stay only in the identification stage, you will need an external stimulus to help you identify something. Can you imagine walking around with a feeling list in your phone such that whenever someone asked you how you were feeling, you would have to get your phone out and scroll through the list until you found an emotion that fit your feeling?

Hadassah not only could identify a letter or word, she would speak her letters and words to someone. She spent hours looking into her mom's and dad's eyes, communicating her letters and words. She was identifying and then communicating these words to another human being. This communication accelerated Hadassah's ability to integrate her first language.

Computer software programs geared toward teaching a language encourage the learner to speak the words as he or she learns them. Ideally, the fastest way to learn a language is immersion. Many mission organizations use immersion to accelerate the missionary's language integration into their new culture.

Immersion is simply speaking the new language to real people; even better, speaking your new language to people more skilled in that language than you are. This process of communicating language accelerates your language ability as your brain integrates language at a much higher rate and level than if you sit in class studying how to identify a word.

Some of you may be thinking that the objective of this book is to study emotions. This is partially true. Another key objective of this book is to communicate feelings to another person, at will. You will be getting an opportunity and experience of a lifetime, becoming able to identify and communicate emotions to just about anyone.

Taking the time and effort to share your feelings with a real person will bring decades of rewards. Your feelings may happen internally, but they are experienced in the context of relationship. After all, what benefit would come from telling your feelings to a rock? A rock cannot feel back, experience feelings with you, mirror back to you your emotions, nor take you by the arm so you can go deeper. No, rocks cannot do this, but a person with a heartbeat and willingness to hear can do all this as you become emotionally fit.

The exercise we will discuss is similar to getting a workout partner. I have worked out most of my life, and there have been times when I lifted weights by myself. As I look back, I realize those periods were just okay. They were not nearly as good as when I had a workout partner or personal trainer.

When I work out with others, I glean several benefits. First, I am accountable to show up and work out. This alone moves me from an emotionally based to a principle based workout time. Second, I learn a lot. My last trainer brought skills to the table that took my workouts to a much more intelligent and effective place. Third, when I have a workout partner who is considerably stronger than me, it pushes me to go farther than I would have by myself. His intensity and focus help me accelerate my workouts.

Having someone you can share your feelings with is like having a workout partner. This partner can help you stay accountable to do your feelings communication exercise daily so you make steady progress. If this person is even slightly ahead of you emotionally, he or she can encourage you to go farther than you would if you were trying to do this alone.

I realize this might take some courage and you might want to keep your emotions buried deep inside, afraid to let them see the light of day. I have watched thousands do this step and no one has died, nor have they regretted putting themselves out there emotionally.

Before we get started, I want to briefly explore the benefits of communicating your feelings to encourage you to take that first emotional step outside of yourself.

Benefits

The first benefit to communicating your emotions with a real person is the improvement of your ability to identify your emotions. I have witnessed countless clients pick an emotion off the list, and as they start to share that emotion, actually correct themselves and recategorize the feeling.

For example, Jerry started to share his example of being alone when his dad did not pick him up. As he shared this feeling to his wife, he corrected himself: "That's not alone; that's unimportant." Had he just written this emotion down, he might not have self-corrected and identified what he was actually feeling.

The second benefit of communicating your feelings with someone is connectivity. Although we do not know exactly where feelings are located in the human body, the one thing for sure is they are not felt in our brains. When you identify feelings, you are limited to how you think you feel as opposed to feeling the feeling.

When you communicate a feeling to a person, you are much more likely to connect to the emotion you are sharing. Right then, in real time, you are not thinking a feeling; you are actually feeling the emotion.

I use the feelings communication exercise often in my 3- and 5-Day Intensives. Almost every time one or both spouses will "bump" into a feeling. He or she will express an emotion and suddenly start having the feeling in the presence of the spouse.

For many couples, it is the first time or the first time in a long time they have actually experienced a feeling together. When you communicate your feelings with another person, you actually might feel the feeling during your communication exercise. This feeling is a big step forward on your journey to emotional fitness.

The third benefit of feeling communication is the experience of engaging your body. When you communicate your feeling and feel the feeling you are accomplishing a significant internal task as well. You are actually achieving a better, internal location and filing this emotion. Your body will remember experiencing this feeling. This is important because, in the future when you feel this feeling, oftentimes it is felt in your body first.

This refined internal connection and ability to locate a feeling is a gift you receive as you practice your feelings communication exercise with another person. This internal retrieval of emotional memory is a result of an organic emotion maturing that you will need in the future as you locate and feel an emotion before you actually expand those.

The final benefit is huge, though it might seem a bit abstract at first, when communicating your emotions. When you open up emotionally and communicate your feelings to another soul, eye-to-eye, you are being beheld. Your emotions are who you are in that very moment. You are not sharing a fact or theory; you are sharing you. When you share you in the presence of another, you are experiencing being beheld.

Being beheld can be awkward or even uncomfortable at first. However, as you practice, you can experience one of the greatest joys of being human: the joy of being known by another, by being beheld by them.

I truly believe that being beheld is a core desire of all humans. However, it is hard to let someone behold you unless you are emotionally available in that moment. I know that what I am describing may be outside of your current experience, but my hope is, as you work through this process, you will be comfortable and confident in your emotional self. You will embrace a lifestyle that includes the experience of being beheld and the joy of beholding others.

Right Person

I am about to share with you how to do the emotions communication exercise, but talking about finding the right person to do this exercise with is key. A few characteristics are necessary in this person.

Willingness is the first characteristic. If someone is not willing or desiring, they might sabotage you during your exercise. They may not make themselves available consistently, which will send the message that your healing is not important to them. They may also be closed off during the exercise, making it difficult or painful for you as you express your emotions. Do not pick someone you need to strong-arm into meeting together.

Someone who is available is necessary. This exercise is done face-to-face. Make sure this person can commit to the ten or fifteen minutes it takes to do the exercise.

Honesty is another important quality for the person with whom you will do this exercise. People who are unable to be honest will likely be shallow when doing the feelings communication exercise with you, due to their fear of emotional intimacy or being known.

A person able to keep confidence is the final quality we will discuss. A person who shares your personal information or brings up your personal stuff when they are mad at you is not a safe person with whom to do this exercise.

If you are married and your spouse is a reasonable person and willing to take this journey with you, I would highly recommend that you choose him or her as your communication partner. Couples who can identify and communicate feelings have a much stronger, more intimate relationship than those who do not, or who struggle with these skills. If you choose your spouse as communication partner, make sure you refrain from providing examples about each other when doing the feelings communication exercise.

Your spouse should never hear, "I feel frustrated when you..." You can feel frustrated about the children, neighbors, friends, politics, or potholes, but no examples about your spouse, not even when you are doing positive feelings.

If your spouse is unwilling or significantly unsafe, pick another person of the same gender. Sharing your feelings across gender will build intimacy outside your marriage and a significant threat to your marriage can develop.

If you are doing emotional fitness as a group, then choose anyone of the same gender who can meet regularly. If you are dating someone, this person would also be an option. You will develop stronger feelings toward this person, so make sure you want to be connected to them if you do this.

A friend of the same gender who is up for a little bit of a journey can also be a good choice. You may also select a person of the same gender in a support group with which you may be connected. A safe spiritual leader from your spiritual community may also be an excellent choice. Often, these people are very open to you growing, so you may find support there.

Lastly, if you honestly cannot find someone, hire a therapist with whom you can do the feelings communication exercise. Let the therapist know that you only want to share your feelings, not process every emotion, since that is not the purpose of the exercise.

Rules

There are a few very important rules for the emotions communication exercise. The rules apply regardless of the person with whom you choose to do this exercise.

Rule One: When you do the emotions communication exercise, never use an example that involves the other person. You might be tempted to do a positive feeling about them. Do not, under any circumstances, use them as an example in your exercise. If you break this rule, it can rapidly deteriorate the effectiveness of the exercise. Doing this can become unsafe if you or the other person unloads, limiting your ability to feel safe when doing this exercise.

Outside of the exercise, you can talk about feelings about your relationship. However, do not do this right after the exercise either. Pick a time separate from the emotions communication exercise to discuss emotions in your relationship.

Rule Two: Maintain eye contact when sharing your feelings with the other person and when you are listening to the other person share his feelings. Try to be present and actively listen. Remember, this person is not just sharing an emotion; she is sharing herself with you. This is a kind of sacred trust, so keep eyes open and listen actively.

Rule Three: Provide absolutely no feedback. You are not to comment, ask questions, or try to get clarification when you are listening. You are only listening. This rule allows both of you to be safe. Immediate feedback can injure the exercise and limit its effectiveness.

Rule Four: The 72-hour rule. Do not discuss what either of you have shared with each other during the exercise for at least seventy-two hours. This rule keeps you safe from instant curiosity or investigation.

If you are still thinking about something seventy-two hours later, then discuss what was shared.

The emotions communication exercise is designed to help a person communicate. It is not about processing emotions. Attempts to process these emotions all the time will absolutely sabotage the exercise.

At this stage of emotional fitness, we are walking, not running. If someone wants to make this exercise a therapy session, this person may not be the right person with whom to do this exercise on an ongoing basis.

The Exercise

It was important for me to prep you before this exercise because it is a big step for many in moving toward emotional fitness.

Step One: Select an emotion you have already used in the emotions identification exercise. If you have not done this exercise yet, take a moment to pick an emotion and complete the two sentences below.

I feel _____ when _____.

I first remember feeling _____ when _____.

When you both have completed the exercise using two different emotion words, you are ready.

Step Two: Look at your sentences. Get a feel for what you are going to share. Then look at the other person and share your first sentence.

Providing and accepting no feedback, let the other person share his first feeling (both sentences), then repeat it so both of you have done at least two separate feeling words each.

If you are meeting less than daily, repeat the exercise with more than two feeling words each. If you have both written out your feelings prior to doing the communication exercise, the exercise will be effective and less time consuming.

If at all possible, work your way through the entire emotions list. Over time, you will absolutely be amazed at what you will learn about yourselves and each other.

On the following page is a log to help you keep track of how many emotions you share with this person over the next ninety days.

Externalized Emotions

My family and I love to watch movies together. They inspire, instruct, and even warn us about principles of life. One particular scene from one of the original Star Wars movies, one in which young Luke Skywalker is being trained by Obi-Wan Kenobi, illustrates this point. In his training, Obi-Wan challenges Luke to use his light saber to hit a ball moving in all different directions. Luke struggles to hit the moving ball until Obi-Wan suggests something completely out of the box for young Skywalker to try.

Luke is instructed to put on a blindfold so he cannot see. At first, Luke doubts the wisdom of Obi-Wan, but acquiesces to his training method. Luke begins to internally sense the moving ball's location. He starts to master this internal sense until it is more accurate than his sight. After his success, he is able to see Obi-Wan's wisdom. Luke was looking for external perception to hone his warrior skills. He did not know that his internal skills were what really needed honing.

One day, Barb walked into my office. Barb is thirty-five, though you would never guess this because of how well she takes care of herself, externally. She has made many mistakes in her life, including a numbing addiction and poor choices in men. She is married to a successful, handsome man who travels frequently. Unfortunately, he cheated on Barb, and they are in my office to try and put things back together.

She is rightfully hurt and angry about the infidelity. As we go deeper into Barb's personal issues, she is able to externalize almost everything. Taking a verbal trip through her relationship, she is able to see that she had become the female version of each key man in her life. She felt she did not know who she really is.

Emotionally, Barb is also very external. She puts total responsibility for how she feels on her husband. He dictated how she felt about herself. It took Barb time to work through some of the exercises in this book, but she did. Once she did the work, she was able to find herself, where she was, and what she felt. Once Barb could locate herself, she was able to find her own voice; she was able to take responsibility for her own abandonment and establish boundaries to move forward with her husband while keeping her own value.

Clark and Kim are another highly successful couple with which I've worked. Years ago, Clark had several affairs. To his credit, he aggressively dealt with his infidelity, sexual addiction, and intimacy anorexia. Kim also did some serious recovery on her intimacy anorexia and attended group for a few years.

Clark and Kim were moving along fine, but periodically, I would get a call. They would be at each other's throats again, and the fights were getting more out of control and more ugly. Both Clark and Kim had the same problem, but did not know it. They were both externalizing a particular feeling which was leading them back to a cycle of disrespecting each other and fighting like two adolescent siblings. The feeling they were both externalizing was fear.

During the beginning stages of their relationship, Kim made several passionate threats to leave Clark if he were unfaithful. This threat was extremely difficult for Clark since they had been together since high school. Clark kept hold of that fear even years later, and he resented Kim for it. Remember, Kim chose to stay with Clark and work on the marriage. In fact, Kim did not leave him—not even for a day—as a result of his infidelity. However, Clark's externalized fear (blaming her for his feeling of fear) prevented him from fully connecting with Kim. It caused him to push her away and blame her for his negative behavior.

Kim was also externalizing her fear. Kim had a deep fear that Clark would cheat on her again. Her external fear (blaming him for her fear), likewise, prevented her from fully giving herself to him and caused her to blame him for her lack of connecting. Clark had passed numerous polygraphs verifying he was not only no longer cheating, but also not looking at porn, masturbating, or talking to other women inappropriately. Both Kim and Clark's fears were ungrounded.

They both had fear, but were externalizing their fear. Once both of them could understand fear was an internal issue, they could remove the fear from their hearts and their relationship.

Externalizing

People who generally externalize their feelings share a certain set of characteristics. This cluster of characteristics, seen here and there without identification, could appear random or even to be an aspect of these people's personalities. However, when you see this cluster identifiably together, you are most likely dealing with or are in a relationship with an externalizer. Listed below are the characteristics externalizers tend to have in common.

1. Not Responsible

An externalizer somehow has feelings happen to them. They do not have a clue why they feel the way they do almost all of the time. I think we all experience this from time to time, however, the externalizer lives with regular cycles of emotions bubbling up, suppressing them, and sometimes exploding with them.

When you ask externalizers why they are acting a certain way, they often respond by telling you they do not know. If you ask if they had a choice regarding their feelings or behavior, they often become confused or defensive. At their core, they do not believe they are responsible for their feelings. This childlike emotional development is challenging to live with since they cannot predict an emotion or know how expansive it is going to get. It is the classic feeling of, *Here we go again.* Their externalizing will become very identifiable to you as you become more emotionally fit.

2. Others Make Them Feel

Since the method of control is believed to be outside of the externalizer, others make this person feel whatever they are feeling. This might be other people specifically or generally, and might be due to circumstances or even abstract groups of people.

The externalizer believes you make them feel angry, insecure, or whatever emotion they are experiencing. So what you do outside the externalized emotional person causes their feelings. This dynamic can also work with positive emotions and affect thought, too. The externalizer can feel appreciated or loved based upon what another person does or says to them.

A classic line that exposes this characteristic might go something like this: "You make me so mad." If you have a friend, spouse, coworker, or family member who repeatedly uses this line, he or she is most likely an externalized emotional person.

Sadly, this person's emotions can go all over the map, depending on the circumstances or the people with whom he or she interacts. They appear (and actually are) fragile and emotionally unstable. Fortunately, this tendency becomes less true once they learn to become emotionally fit.

3. Blame

If others make you feel whatever you are feeling, then it is perfectly logical to blame them for your feelings. The externalized person feels he gets to blame others or blame circumstances.

An externalized person is angry because you made him angry. He is afraid because you made him afraid. Sadly enough, the externalizer will almost always blame others for his less than positive feelings, but may not as often attribute his positive feelings to others.

4. Victim

When you live in a world where others control how you feel and act, you not only get to blame them, you get to play the role of victim. Since you are constantly being jerked around by others' control of your emotions, you feel you are a victim—a victim of your spouse, your family, and your friends.

You are a victim of television shows, news, and politics. If you hear a lot of self-victimizing from someone around you, she is most likely an externally focused, emotional person. If you even suggest she is responsible for her own feelings or reactions, you will most likely get quite an earful as to why this is not true for her.

5. Critical

Criticism is commonly found in those whose method of emotional control is mostly external. The externalized person tends to focus on weaknesses or unfavorable attributes of a person or group.

This behavior may help the externalizer justify his inappropriate feelings of rage, hurt, prejudice, and unforgiveness toward a person or group of people. The externalized emotional person is quick to see what is wrong with others and tends to see people more in a static way (like a photograph) than as a process (like a movie). Their judgments tend to be quick and their emotional responses to those of whom they are critical are, of course, the other person's fault.

6. Easily Offended

If others are responsible for your feelings, you could be easily offended. The emotionally externalized person finds offense like a lint brush finds lint. If there is even a small reason for discomfort, disagreement, or dislike, the externalized person can be offended.

I see a lot of externalized emotional people in the airport. Recently, I watched such a person when his flight (the same one I was on) was delayed in Chicago. As I watched the crowd, I could tell those that were externalized, based on their reaction to the delay. It is as if someone told them they were fat, ugly, and stupid. I sat calmly because I had come into the situation knowing that the odds of flying out of Chicago on time were especially bad.

The tendency to be easily offended can show up in any environment: home, work, school, or other. This tendency can show up in any and all relationships. If you happen to be in a relationship with an externalized emotional person, relax. You are in no way responsible for his feelings or how he chooses to express his feelings. His reaction is not personal, and there is hope if he chooses to become emotionally fit.

7. Primitive Responses

I have spent many years around teenagers and noticed that due to their hormones and emotions, they tend to display primitive emotional responses. Their intensity is high. They might yell, slam a door, get loud, or curse. They might be abrupt, rude, or cruel. Usually, after a little while, they acknowledge their extreme responses and apologize. I find that externalized emotional people display similarly primitive and intense emotional expressions on a fairly regular basis. If you are around such a person regularly, you never know what is going to happen. These primitive responses seem somewhat childish and often self-focused. This is due to a lack of skill and control of emotions (all of which can greatly improve as the process of emotional fitness is applied). Even at the end of the 60-Day Journal (found at the end of this book), I see a dramatic shift in primitive responses.

8. Anger/Sadness

I can totally relate here. When I was more externalized, I used anger and sadness, as many externalizers do.

Anger is a huge catchall for any strong emotion. Strong emotions like confusion, frustration, and misunderstanding get confused and communicated as anger. The emotionally externalized person can so overuse anger that people may describe him or her as an angry person. I choose to think of these people as less skilled or emotionally constipated.

Sadness can also be a catchall for stronger feelings that have yet to be identified or mastered in any significant manner. If the externalized person feels unvalued, discounted, alone, lonely, etc., they tend to express the emotion as sadness. Sometimes this externalized person cannot tell you why she feels sad; she just does. As in the case of anger, she can become more emotionally fit, needing sadness less and less.

9. Gullible

Since emotions are externalized, a person can be easily manipulated.

A simple comment about how smart, attractive, hardworking, creative, well-dressed, or how good of a person or parent he is can make an externalized person turn off all reason. He feels *they like me.* Once an externally emotional person feels liked, loved, appreciated, wanted, noticed, or seen by another person, he will then like and want to be around that person.

This makes externally emotional people very susceptible to those who want to manipulate or use them. As pointed out earlier, the externally emotional person ascribes people on the outside for how he feels. If a person can make him feel very positive, then he becomes gullible or more easily influenced.

When I travel I occasionally get time to do some shopping. I have noticed that retail stores have picked up on what I am explaining to you. When you walk in, you are given no casual greeting. Instead, the salesperson comments about your tie, jacket, shoes, or some other item you have on. Instantly, you feel desirable, smart, approved of— even validated. Then when you pick up an item, she is quick to tell you how great a choice you made, or that she has that same item held for herself in the back.

The externally motivated person can easily be taken for a positive ride and find himself not only making purchases, but returning to the same store for that positive feeling. This same dynamic can apply to relationships as well. Since others make him feel a certain way, he can even return to a bad, illicit, or financially, emotionally, inequitable relationship to feel a certain way.

10. Prone to Medicate

You can imagine living a life where others seem to be controlling your emotions. Some of your emotional lack of control and intense or inappropriate expressions of feelings make for a painful way to live.

Ongoing pain in the emotionally externalized person will cause a desire to medicate in some way. Suppose you had a toothache; this mild pain will demand that you take something for the pain. If you ignore the source of your toothache, it gets worse. Your body will tell you to either take more of the same pain medication or take something stronger.

The soul of the externalized emotional person has something to do with the pain in which they find themselves. This pain often starts off small, as feeling different and separate, but can get deeper as the person moves toward feeling rejected, unwanted, unworthy, or unacceptable.

Depending on access to medicines, she can choose food, masturbation, porn, alcohol, drugs, codependency, caffeine, sugar, exercise, work, and spending or making money. The list goes on and on. Herein is a significant future problem for the soul that is externalized emotionally. The pain remains constant and, over time, more intense unless the person becomes more emotionally fit. Without intervention that leads to emotional fitness, the medicine becomes used more and more until it becomes a problem as well. I know many people on their way to emotional fitness who have had to address the roadblock of addiction.

If you know someone who is medicating her abuse, neglect, or trauma, the medicine will have to be addressed. I have seen amazing results with those who combined the emotional fitness program with their recovery from their medicine of choice.

11. Passive/Aggressive

The last characteristic of the externalized emotional person is a relationship style I have seen repeatedly in two extreme relationship styles. The first style is passive. In this style the individual thinks less of himself and overvalues others. This person usually has weak boundaries and takes more dysfunction from others than he should. Generally, this dynamic indicates a lack of love, honor, and respect toward himself. This person will easily be controlled by what someone else thinks or supposedly thinks of him.

The second style of relating is aggressive. This person thinks more of himself and thinks less of others. This person is more likely to try to control others through anger or withholding love. He or she struggles to see the value of other people and therefore lacks love, honor, and respect toward them. Usually this person thinks in context of *What can you do for me?* and will tend to emotionally bully those around him.

We have just explored the externalized emotional person. You may know someone you identify as such, or seen yourself in the previous pages. To make this easier for you to assess, I have listed the characteristics below.

1. Not responsible   ___ Yes ___ No

2. Others make them feel   ___ Yes ___ No

3. Blame   ___ Yes ___ No

4. Victim   ___ Yes ___ No

5. Critical   ___ Yes ___ No

6. Easily offended   ___ Yes ___ No

7. Primitive responses   ___ Yes ___ No

8. Anger/Sadness   ___ Yes ___ No

9. Gullible   ___ Yes ___ No

10. Prone to medicate   ___ Yes ___ No

11. Passive/Aggressive   ___ Yes ___ No

As you honestly check off the Yes/No boxes for yourself, what is your score? If you scored three or more of these externalized characteristics as a Yes, you may be struggling with externalizing your emotions. The greater the number of Yes responses, the greater the struggle for you or the person with whom you are in a relationship.

You probably had some awareness on this issue, but lacked the language to understand this in your life. I would like to congratulate you because you are reading the right book to help you move from where you are to becoming a much more emotionally fit person.

The development you can see in yourself and your relationships can be tremendous. Keep reading and doing the work I suggest. Then you will be able to truly congratulate yourself.

One other thing that can be helpful in allowing yourself to see the externalizing pattern in you is that you will also gain the ability to see others in your life who are emotionally externalized. I put together a list of relationships that might apply to you, below. You can indicate your responses to these questions on a separate sheet of paper if you wish to keep your answers confidential.

Externalized People in My Life

Spouse   ____ Yes ____ No

Parents   ____ Yes ____ No

Children   ____ Yes ____ No

Coworkers   ____ Yes ____ No

Boss   ____ Yes ____ No

Friends   ____ Yes ____ No

When you look at the primary people in your life, what percentage of them fit an externalized profile? _____%

As you look at your life, do you tend to attract these people?

Do you feel this externalizer profile deserves you at this current time?

Having a new paradigm can help you see yourself and others from a different perspective. You shouldn't necessarily tell them what you're learning; the information is largely for your use. As you become more emotionally fit, you will naturally tend to attract more emotionally fit people into your life.

Internalized Emotions

Let us return for a moment to the example of Luke Skywalker. Remember how he was dependent on the external to get the job done and was failing miserably? When he switched gears to rely on his internal perception, he was able to accurately hit the ball and hit it every time.

Before I start to outline the internalized emotional person, I want to share this thought: People are gifted in different areas. We can see this truism clearly as we go through school. There are the really smart kids, the ones who do not have to study to get straight A's, but then on the other side of the classroom there are kids who have to study just to get average grades. There are the gifted athletes who are superior to everyone else in almost any sport, but also kids who love sports and try hard, but are just average at them. There are the socially gifted kids who naturally attract and maintain friends, but then there are those who cannot seem to fit in or figure out social rules. There are also the artists, dancers, musicians and others who are innately gifted in the arts while others struggle.

Reading the last chapter on externalized emotional people, you were able to identify a similar range of abilities. There are people on both sides of the spectrum as well as many in the middle. There are some people who are innately emotionally developed. They may have been born with a gift. They may have gone to therapy early on and been exposed to emotional skills and actually utilized these tools as they developed.

However, like our friends in high school, they would be quite the minority in western culture. We should celebrate these people's giftedness and at the same time celebrate the fact that people can work to become very emotionally fit.

As previously mentioned, my son Jubal played football. He wanted to play on the front line, defense and offense. Though he was not blessed with extreme height or weight, he was blessed with determination and discipline. I have never seen another player get by my son—he just stays on them. Some teams would even double-team him on defense. He probably had more quarterback sacks than any other lineman in his division—even several in one game—earning him his division's first team choice, as voted on by other coaches in his division.

My son never looked at what he did not have; he looked at what he did have and utilized his determination and disciplines to learn and master better technique, utilizing 100 percent of the force he could muster, surprising many of the bigger kids who never had to give 100 percent.

I'm saying this to illustrate the truth that if you apply hard work and discipline, it will not matter if you scored ten or eleven in the last chapter on externalized emotions, you can move to a more internalized understanding of managing your emotions. As you apply the principles that follow, your emotional fitness can shift not only the way you relate to yourself but also the very location of these emotions, if they are more internal or external.

Characteristics of the Emotionally Internalized

The characteristics of an emotionally internalized person can be clearly seen. With the externalized person, it is as if there is a zipper tag on the outside of them for others to control, whereas the internalizer's tag is on the inside. As we walk through the characteristics, you will get a clear idea who these people are and how to recognize them. You may even be surprised to see that those in your life may be more internalized emotionally than you once thought.

1. Responsible for Their Emotions

Emotional internalizers accept full responsibility for what they are feeling. The emotions they have are their emotions, unlike those of Clark and Kim who externalized their fears. For example, an internalized spouse would say, "I have some fear and take responsibility for that emotion."

In their relationships, others are not responsible for how they feel. They do not blame others or feel as if they are victims of others, generally speaking. This shift of personal responsibility of emotions is a major indicator of an internalized emotional person. They are not people who look to others or the environment for why they feel the way they do.

2. Emotions Are a Choice

One of the amazing features of internalized emotional people is their neuropathic ability to choose how they feel about someone or something. It's like their emotional processes allow them to say, "I could feel X, Y, or Z about this situation, and I choose Y."

Erica was a young professional who had dated a man she worked with. They had dated for a few months and then broke off the relationship. Talking to Erica at a social gathering, I offered my condolences to the lost relationship. Erica looked me straight in the eyes and clearly and confidently said, "I could have gotten all down and sulky about it, but really, I feel great knowing he's not the right one, and I'm one guy closer to finding the right one."

I've been around my share of young women who experience breakups. Most don't choose how they feel about it. Erica processed her emotions internally, looked at her options, and chose how she wanted to feel.

Choosing emotions for most of us is a skill we have to learn, a skill that the following chapters will help teach. However, Erica, like most internalized emotional people, just gets that feelings are a choice. Such people might feel down, but they decide that accepting this sad feeling may not be the best choice and then choose to feel differently.

Some people are able to do this choosing easily. For them it is a gift— an innate ability. For others, the ability might come through practice. You get there when you accept your feelings are fully a choice, and herein, you have more power in your life.

3. Chooses Responses

Internalizers choose how they feel about something emotionally. They have the ability to choose how to respond emotionally to a person or situation.

A situation occurs and the internalizer feels something initially, decides how she wants to feel about the situation, and then chooses a response. She does not react to the situation like an externalizer might.

This ability gives the internalizer quite a bit of power and influence in a situation or relationship. Phillip and Tami have been married for twelve years. They have a history of getting angry with each other and exploding, calling names, and being generally disrespectful of each other. Phillip has been practicing his emotional fitness program for almost two months. He expressed how Tami was still going off in her anger, but he was able to stay with his feelings and switch to respect and empathy. He talked about how he could stay calm, help her figure out what she was really feeling so she could settle down, and then helped them both get somewhere.

Phillip was learning how to choose his feelings and then his responses. As he chose his response, instead of reacting like he did in the past, Phillip was able to effectively change the outcome of an ongoing problem in their marriage that had lasted several years.

4. Looks Inside

An emotional internalizer knows that feelings are located within. When faced with a difficult emotion, an internalizer does not jump outside of himself to blame or criticize.

The internalizer will ask himself questions as to why he is feeling what he is feeling. He will acknowledge he is feeling afraid, insecure, or "less than." Then he will ask why. *What is going on inside of me that is causing this feeling to come up?* He asks if this feeling is triggering something in the past that he needs to address.

The internalized emotional adult does not fear the internal journey. He knows the emotion is inside and can be explored, so he explores it. Often, he is able to discover a reason and decide what he wants to do with that emotion.

5. Grows

Internalizers take the journey inside and ask the questions we just discussed. Because they take the journey, they can discover a past family of origin issue, a sibling issue, a past romantic issue, and understand why the connection between the issue and the emotion.

If the issue needs to be addressed, they often take steps to address it. This insight and ability to take responsible action causes the internalizer to grow as a result of experiencing a strong or challenging feeling. Consistent growth, year after year, allows this person to apply the emotionally fit principles to keep herself on an expedient emotional growth process.

6. Honest

For the most part, emotional internalizers are very honest about how they feel. They know an emotion is just an emotion. They do not tend to suffer from embarrassment or shame for having an emotion.

They might not always be proud of how they feel, but they are usually honest with themselves and others about what they are feeling. For the internalizer, a feeling is just a feeling, not good or bad.

7. Fearless

The internalizers do not fear their emotions. They are not afraid an emotion is going to sweep them off their feet and carry them to a place they do not want to go.

They know they are responsible for how they feel and they can manage almost any emotion that comes up. They have experience in reigning in the intensity of an emotion, switching an emotion, and not fearing it. They are generally fearless about their responses. They are more confident because they can weed out what they are feeling, choose to feel, and respond at will.

This fearlessness is strikingly difference from what an externalizer exhibits. This type of person, because of this skill set alone, can find himself leading because he leads himself emotionally.

8. Assertive

In the last chapter I explored passive (less respect for self) and assertive (less respect for others). Emotional internalizers are assertive. They respect themselves and how they feel, and also fully respect others and what they might be feeling. Emotional internalizers do not need to bully you if you disagree, but they will not be bullied or intimidated by anyone either.

They know who they are inside and give respect and honor to others. They also expect honor as they express their emotions and thoughts.

9. Equal

In my experience in meeting with emotional internalizers all over the globe, they all seem to live out one major core idea or belief that influences all their relationships. At their core, deep down inside, they believe everyone is equal. Everyone has equal value, regardless of status, accomplishments, position, education, or abilities.

A soul is valuable, period. For the internalized emotional person, this is a settled issue. They can talk to any person, regardless of who they are or what they do. They acknowledge people. You can feel they are present with you when you speak to them. Seeing others as equal is a great strength for anyone to possess.

10. Apologizes

When was the last time a spouse, friend, family member, or coworker apologized to you? When was the last time you received such an apology without an argument, threat, or request (or demand) for a return apology? You may be struggling to recall an instance of someone apologizing to you—much more so to recall someone doing so without threat, argument, or request for a return apology.

I have done this and it is quite refreshing. I assessed the situation, realized I had made a mistake, and chose to take responsibility, without shame.

This type of interaction comes mostly from emotionally internalized people. Such a one is capable of this because he generally takes responsibility, separates it from feelings of shame or embarrassment, chooses to feel human, flawed, and still loved, and corrects the error.

The ability to apologize is probably one of the highest indicators of emotional health. The harder it is for an individual to apologize, the stronger his or her need for emotional fitness.

11. Empowering

The last characteristic of emotional internalizers I would like to explore here is their subtle (though sometimes not so subtle) ability to empower others. They are not threatened by your strengths or abilities because they see you as equal in value. They can congratulate, give you creative ideas to solve problems, and even assist you without recognition.

With a kind word, acknowledgment of the efficiently of a task, or general attitude of appreciation, the emotional internalized person empowers others around her. You notice you feel better when you are around her. By whom do you feel empowered? To whom can you entrust something and find her competence and attitude refreshing? She just might be an emotional internalizer.

In these last few pages, we have explored the emotional internalizer. You might be thinking I am talking about someone who does not exist. Trust me, in a couple months, you just might be more like this internalizer than you can imagine.

Listed below are eleven characteristics of an emotional internalized person. Check off Yes or No to represent yourself as you are today. I want you to be brutally honest with yourself. If this is challenging for you, ask a spouse or friend you trust to see what they think, but do your best to be authentic.

1. Responsible for their emotions ____ Yes ____ No

2. Feelings are a choice ____ Yes ____ No

3. Chooses responses ____ Yes ____ No

4. Looks inside ____ Yes ____ No

5. Grows emotionally ____ Yes ____ No

6. Honest with self and feelings ____ Yes ____ No

7. Fearless ____ Yes ____ No

8. Assertive ____ Yes ____ No

9. Equal ____ Yes ____ No

10. Apologizes ____ Yes ____ No

11. Empowering ____ Yes ____ No

As you read on and do the emotional fitness program, you are going to grow emotionally at an exponential rate. At this point, you might not be sure you can change, but I have watched many emotionally challenged and externalized individuals, both men and women, dramatically change. I truly believe in this process.

Here is what I would like you to do. After you have finished reading this book and practiced the emotionally fit program for sixty days, I want you to come back and check off the Yes and No's that apply to you at that time. I believe you will see a fantastic difference.

Internalized List—60 Days into Emotional Fitness Program

1. Responsible for their feelings   ____ Yes ____ No

2. Feelings are a choice   ____ Yes ____ No

3. Chooses responses   ____ Yes ____ No

4. Looks inside   ____ Yes ____ No

5. Grows   ____ Yes ____ No

6. Honest   ____ Yes ____ No

7. Fearless   ____ Yes ____ No

8. Assertive   ____ Yes ____ No

9. Equal   ____ Yes ____ No

10. Apologizes   ____ Yes ____ No

11. Empowering   ____ Yes ____ No

Object vs. Being

Emotional fitness can be challenging. Many find it hard to identify and communicate feelings, connect their body to feelings, and struggle with addictions.

There is another challenge that is also important to undertake. If this relates to you, it will be very important for you to identify and address as you move toward emotional fitness. If this challenge does not apply to you, it will be helpful for you to read this chapter anyway because it may explain those with who you have been in relationship.

None of us can choose our families or the events that occur in our lives. Sue is an example of not being able to choose the events that happen to us. She is a bright, thirty-two-year-old who works in the technology industry as a computer programmer. Her parents got married at age nineteen and became pregnant with her at age twenty-one. Sue's parents had a reputation for being partiers. They regularly got high, drunk, went to concerts and parties, and spent most of their free time plastered. Eventually their partying led to cheating, lots of anger, chaos, and a few separations while Sue was growing up.

One night when Sue was twelve, her parents had a party. In typical fashion, they both passed out. That night a stranger entered Sue's room and raped her. He told her that if she told anyone, he would come back and kill her parents. She then started to self-medicate. She spiraled out of control. She could party, but she could not connect with men. Before she was twenty years old, she had been pregnant twice and terminated both pregnancies.

Sue then had a deep spiritual change and stopped partying, cleaned up her life, and married a man who later became a pastor. Her life looks very good on the outside. She has a steady job, a ministry in her church, and two great children, but she has trouble connecting in her life.

Jacob has a story totally different from Sue's. He grew up in a stable, traditional Jewish home.

When talking with Jacob, he often praises his parents for how educated, hardworking, and successful they are. His mom is a doctor and his dad is a lawyer. In his family, emotional connection and feelings were not discussed. They were considered irrelevant, and their expression was seen as weakness. Jacob felt the brunt of this because he had a sensitive heart, but would be condemned anytime he showed his feelings at home.

Jacob married an expressive Italian named Marcy, and together they are raising four handsome boys. Jacob has the same problem as Sue. He cannot connect, especially to Marcy.

How is it possible that two people from opposite spectrums of life have the same problem? To survive or get their needs met, they have to be different than themselves. They have to become not someone else but something else.

Many people reading these pages will identify with this difficulty. It happens when there is little to no connection in a family. It can also happen when there is a trauma, severe neglect, or abandonment. These situations can cause a person to conclude that it is not okay to be him or herself.

The Object

Sometimes people become objects in order to survive emotionally. As an object, they can project anything they want to those around them in an attempt to be accepted and survive.

Jacob became an object and projected being smart and hardworking because he knew that behavior would be accepted and approved by his parents. Sue partied, which was totally against who she was as a person, to protect herself from being raped again.

Becoming an object can happen incrementally, like it did for Jacob. He concluded he would not be accepted if he was himself, so he gave his parents the child he thought they wanted. Becoming an object can also happen immediately if you are used as an object by someone in an abuse situation.

As an object, you will have struggles connecting emotionally, especially in romantic relationships. As an object, you will also struggle with being authentic. I want to share with you what an object is and some of the characteristics of a person who chooses to be an object in order to survive.

If you made choices to survive that led you to become an object, your choices might have been the best you could have made at that time. It is important to not feel shame about the choices you made when you were a child or teenager in response to your circumstances. Just like mine, your choices were the best options you could make at the time, given the information you had.

Something I have learned along my personal journey to healing is that those choices I made and things I brought into my life to survive also kept me from living—really living.

As we progress through learning what an object is and what a being is, I want you to absolutely know that you can move from object to being and from surviving to living. Over my career, I have helped many people through this process. My hope is that as you walk through the process, lights will come on and hope will begin to happen for you in a whole new way.

Here is an analogy I use with clients. I take a coaster off my table and hold it between us. I ask the client what it is. She always identifies the item as a coaster. I acknowledge the correct response and add that the item is an object. Like all objects, it can be measured and weighed. As an object, the coaster is limited: it is only so big, it weighs only so much. If I were to break 9 percent of the coaster off in a piece, only 91 percent of it would remain intact. If I remove another percentage of the coaster, even less of it would be intact. Eventually the coaster starts keeping track of the percentage of itself it is losing or giving away and might become resentful.

Below are a few characteristics of people who struggle with being objects.

1. Uncomfortable with their flaws. As an object, you are either all good or all bad. If you are all good by your own measure, you are lovable. If you are flawed, you are all bad and therefore unlovable. You will get angry if others address one of your flaws.

2. Rarely apologize. The object person finds it difficult to believe she can be both flawed and loved. Rather, she believes she is either flawed or loved. Apologizing means she is flawed and puts her into the all bad box; apologizing means she is not loved. Apologies, therefore, are rare and usually come only after much conflict, or with resentment.

3. Measures themselves. The object person measures himself against others. He sees himself as better than or less than for various reasons. Rarely does an object feel truly equal to other beings.

4. They measure their giving. The object person feels she is like a book, so when she gives (especially in marriage or committed relationships) she is ripping out a page of the book. Eventually, she fears she will find herself without pages, empty.

5. Giving is painful. I am not talking about time, gifts, abilities, or money. Giving the heart is painful for an object.

6. Feelings and connecting to feelings are a real challenge. In an object relationship with one's self and others, it is about manipulating images and perspectives to look good or be acceptable. Feelings are an expression of our true self, our being, so this is a challenge for someone who is an object.

7. Tends to read their spouse's and other people's minds, but almost always in the negative. They believe their spouses have certain motives, project those motives onto their spouses, and treat them as if the projection is reality, regardless of the spouses' insistence to the contrary.

8. They tend to relate to themselves and others as functions. People in object relationships tend to see people more for what they do than who they are.

The Matrix movie trilogy is a good example of someone moving from object relationship to valuing others. Neo lives in the object world. He is given the chance to live in the real world and then given the chance to serve real people, and ultimately comes to value other souls enough to give himself totally to their freedom.

I understand the struggle. Moving from object to being has been one of the harder things I have ever done, but I am so glad I did. Because I did, I know almost anyone can do it. It takes work, but it is definitely a way to make progress.

A Being

A being is nothing like an object. A being is absolutely immeasurable in intellect, spirit, desire, experience, history, or personality. As a being, you are not only immeasurable, unfathomable, and unique, but you are also unlimited. My personal belief is that you are eternal.

You are unlimited, and years or decades from now, you will have emotions, spirit, intellect, and energy to have and give away at will.

As a being you can give 10 percent, 20 percent, or more to a spouse, friend, or family member and still have 100 percent of you left. In my experience, when I give, I expand. I can come home after giving to clients and give to my wife, my children, and even my dog, and still have 100 percent of me left.

I am a being and I have almost limitless resources. My resources are replenished daily, and over time, have an opportunity to expand again. I do not feel or keep track of my giving as I give from my being, not as an object. People have inherent, immeasurable value, so it is a privilege to serve and give to them as I can. There is no pain in giving because it is not expensive to give of yourself.

If you are a being already, you totally get what I am saying. If you come from more of an object place, you might be confused. I know what it is like to be an object to myself and others.

Benefits

I gave you characteristics of people who believe they are objects earlier in the chapter. Now I would like to give you some characteristics of people who are beings. Some people are just born this way and stay this way regardless of their life circumstances. Others are nurtured during childhood and adolescence, and being them is the only thing they know. Some of us have to work to get there.

1. Others are equal. Someone who is a being sees others as having value. He is equal to those around him and others are equal to him. Regardless of wealth, accomplishments, or other external measures, he gives true respect to others.

2. Being flawed is being human. She accepts that she can and does make mistakes, and is quick to take responsibility for them. She is not afraid to share it if it will help someone. Mistakes are just part of the learning process of life and self-discovery. She is not less than or less loved because she has flaws.

3. Inquiry before judgment. A being will mostly give people the benefit of the doubt and will inquire as to the reasoning or circumstances surrounding someone's behavior. He sees people more as a whole than as a part and gives grace more often than he does ostracism.

4. Giving is loving. A being gives throughout the day by being present and available. There is no way to track giving; it is just as normal as breathing. If you can help, you do. Recognition is not necessary. It just feels good to serve.

5. Feelings. A being can be authentic in almost any situation. She can share how she feels regardless of the other person's level of maturity. She gives herself permission to be and she provides safety for herself to be authentic.

6. People have value. Regardless of a person's function or direct contribution, people innately have value. How they feel and what they are going through is significant. Compassion for others is a very common characteristic of someone who is a being.

The journey you take to become emotionally fit places you on this growth pattern into being. I wanted to give you a clear picture of what is available to you, so you may, at any point, chose to pull back into your shell.

I believe your true DNA is available and absolutely worth releasing into the world. Your unique DNA can have a very positive influence in this world. You can blossom and become that amazing person you were intended to become. I have committed my life to seeing people reach their true potential.

I really want you to push against anything in the past that would want you to stay an object. There will be a tipping point for you when you will feel you are growing. I believe you can do this amazing work and become the amazing being you were meant to be!

Continuum

I don't want to leave you with an either/or paradigm. I understand that, for whatever reason, you may have needed to become an object in order to survive. There is no pill or event that can switch you instantly from object to being. Fortunately, you move incrementally toward being.

I liken the process to the destiny of a seed. Inside the seed is its own DNA. A sunflower seed becomes a sunflower. Your DNA of being is inside of you and was there way before you had to erect the protective mechanisms around you, moving you toward an object relationship with yourself or others.

I have watched men and women from varying ages, backgrounds, religions, and incomes choose to work and, over time, emerge as immeasurable, unfathomable, amazing, living beings. I have watched this miracle happen so often that I know it can exist for those who go through the growing process.

The seed has to open up, and to do this you have to feel safe. Safety is a gift you give to yourself first, and then seek out people with whom you feel reasonably safe. Notice I said reasonably. Even the purest of hearts and the best of people are not capable of providing perfect safety, and can hurt you. No seed in nature grows without risk of some kind.

You must crack the shell and let out the life in you—the real, authentic you—little by little. It feels hard at first, like the seed pushing through the dirt. As you do it, it may even seem counterintuitive. You must let go of the illusion that the shell keeps you safe. The price you pay for believing in safety is real, so push and push, using the exercises in this book.

Believe me, a day will come when it seems easier to be authentic than to be an object. You are no longer pushing against something; you are growing towards being something. It becomes almost natural to grow. Being authentic and flawed become easier, and being an object feels more and more uncomfortable.

You may lose some relationships with people who want you to stay a seed, but your destiny of growth is getting stronger and stronger. Then your being straightens and you proceed to blossom into whatever amazing being you are supposed to be. You may occasionally remember the days of the seed, but you have no desire to go back.

Roadblocks to Emotional Fitness

As you are traveling the road to becoming more emotionally fit, my hope is that you complete the exercises. Remember, emotional fitness is a result of a known set of disciplines. As you apply these disciplines, more and more you will experience connection to yourself and others. I hope that while you are reading these chapters, you are actively identifying and communicating your emotions to someone. Being proactive will be helpful as you approach the other exercises in future chapters.

In this chapter, I want to make you aware of two major roadblocks that can sabotage your emotional fitness. If either of these two roadblocks are currently part of your life, you will have additional work to become successful emotionally. It also means you have to work a little harder, but the reward is that your results will be much sweeter.

Addiction

For the most part, my career has been dedicated to helping addicts (mostly sexual addicts) get sober and become amazing emotional, spiritual, and moral adults. I see the miracle of recovery from addiction every week.

Having said all that, you must understand a significant side effect to having an addiction: Addicts stop developing emotionally. Regardless if they are a man or woman, and even if chronologically age fifty, most are emotionally aged fourteen to sixteen.

This emotional age represents the time when addictions became active, the response being emotional arrested development. They may be more mature in other areas of their life, but emotionally, they are an adolescent.

In my book, *Intimacy: A 100-Day Guide to Lasting Relationships* (Siloam, 2003), I list the characteristics of an emotional child, adolescent, and adult. Below are corresponding categories.

Feelings	Child	Adolescent	Adult
	doesn't know what you're talking about	has feelings but limited ability to communicate them	has learned how to identify and communicate feelings
	becomes confused when emotions addressed	has periods of emotional constipation, then blows up or gets silent	can be emotionally safe and keep confidences
	feels you're asking too much of them to do feeling work	really more concerned about their feelings than yours	values and hears the feelings of their spouses

Characteristics of Addiction

I am going to briefly go over the 10 commonly associated characteristics of addiction so you can see if addiction may be a possible threat to your emotional fitness. If you come across an area of your life where you are struggling, be honest. If you are honest, you can heal and enjoy a life of freedom.

I am in recovery from several addictions: alcohol, drugs, sex, pornography, caffeine, and sugar. I know better than most what it takes to get and stay free from addictions. Walk through the next few pages with an honest heart and see if you meet enough criteria to consider if recovery from addiction is a needed part of your path to emotional fitness.

1. Try to Stop

In any addiction, you would have made several attempts to stop. You might have even stopped for a day, week, months, or longer, but then you go back to the behavior to which you are addicted. You have some rationalization as to why you go back, but factually you have been unable to stop.

___ Yes ___ No

2. Promise to Stop

When you are addicted, you make several promises to stop the behavior. You might promise yourself. You might promise God, a spouse, a significant other, or a family member. Despite the promises, you return to the behavior.

___ Yes ___ No

3. Consequences

Your addictive behavior or relationships bring into your life some sort of consequence. For some, the consequences are economic; for others, they are relational. Regardless of the type of consequences the addiction has brought into your life, you have paid a price for having this addictive behavior.

___ Yes ___ No

4. Use after Consequences

Even after a significant consequence such as a car accident, loss of a job, loss of a relationship or marriage, you continue to use. You may have had several cycles of consequences, but as you look back, you have continued to use even after each consequence.

___ Yes ___ No

5. Do More

In your addiction, you find yourself increasing more use and abuse of the substance, behavior, or relationship. You started off with just a little bit and now, over time, you see a significant increase of how much you actually abuse the substance, behavior, or relationship.

___ Yes ___ No

6. Tolerance

As an addict, you have an increased tolerance toward a behavior, substance, or relationship. Over time, it takes more of it or a higher form of it to get the same result.

___ Yes ___ No

7. Time

As you look over the past months, years, or decades, you have dedicated more and more of your time to the behavior. This behavior might have started off an hour here and there, but since, it has become more regular.

____ Yes ____ No

8. Withdrawal

If you find yourself unable to access your substance, process, or relationship you experience some form of withdrawal. Your symptoms can swing from crabby to hopeless. You will find this happening almost every time you are in circumstances that last longer than your usage patterns have been in the past.

____ Yes ____ No

9. Decreased Activities

Your addiction, over time, becomes more and more demanding of your time and energy. Over time, you begin to manage your life so there is less time with friends, family, hobbies, spiritual pursuits, and physical activities. As you look back, you can see that you have decreased other activities in your life to accommodate more time for the behavior.

____ Yes ____ No

10. Secret

Most addicts keep their behavior a secret. The primary people in their lives do not know the total truth about how much they are using or doing. They often have secret accounts, cash, passwords, or relationships that supply the substance or process. Having a secret often goes hand in hand with addiction.

____ Yes ____ No

Before you continue, make sure you checked the Yes or No box at the end of each characteristic. If you have checked yes to three or more, you may have an addiction. If you checked more than three, consider that you are addicted to some thing, process, bevavior, substance, or someone.

Here is a short list of common addictions.

Alcohol	Food	Gambling	Drugs
Caffeine	Work	Sex	Sugar
Exercise	Pornography	Shopping	People

If you struggle with an addiction, I recommend you get informed about it. Then join a support group to help you recover. Seek counseling with someone who specializes in that area of addiction recovery. Take the steps you need to address the issues you may be having.

Intimacy Anorexia

Intimacy anorexia is another major roadblock to an emotionally fit lifestyle, and is most destructive to the marriage relationship. Intimacy anorexia is an addiction-like process in which you avoid intimacy with your spouse. First, I want to explain what intimacy anorexia is, then the characteristics of intimacy anorexia. Here are some excerpts from *Intimacy Anorexia: Healing the Hidden Addiction in Your Marriage* (Discovery Press, 2010).

Marriage is the only relationship that, by definition, demands emotional, spiritual, and sexual intimacy on an exclusive, committed basis over a prolonged period of time. As the vow goes, "Til death do us part."

All other relationships can demand some of us, but not all. Even dating relationships can demand all three major aspects, but not in a committed or prolonged basis. The back door is easy to find in dating and harder to find in marriage. This is why intimacy anorexics look normal or even wonderful in the dating process, but on the wedding night or a month or so later, look totally different than in the dating relationship.

Intimacy anorexia can impact other primary relationships, including those with children and extended family. However, it is my experience that it is mostly manifested in the marital relationship.

Intimacy Anorexia is the active withholding of emotional, spiritual, and sexual intimacy from one's spouse.

I think it would be prudent for us to go deeper into the definition of intimacy anorexia so that as we move along and build from here, the foundation of the definition is strong enough to support the weight of the rest of what we are building.

Active: The word "active" is by far the word in the definition of intimacy anorexia most disputed by the anorexics themselves. Everyone around the intimacy anorexic agrees that the word "active" is very appropriate for what they are observing and experiencing. Although it's clear their behaviors of withholding and pushing their spouse away have repeated themselves hundreds or even thousands of times, the intimacy anorexic wants to claim no intention in these behaviors.

In a conversation with a telephone client just the other day, I said, "Let's look at another addiction process that doesn't apply to you."

He agreed.

"Let's talk about an alcoholic who drank for twenty years of his marriage. He would drink, spend money, often become verbally and physically abusive to his wife and family, and neglect many of his responsibilities as a husband and father. Each time he drank, he made a choice to put the bottle in his mouth. Regardless of his family of origin, biochemistry, past abuse, or neglect of his own, he chose to drink. Do you agree?"

"Of course," he said.

"So the alcoholic is responsible for his behavior of drinking, but you are not responsible for withholding?" I asked.

"Oh, I see," he said, sheepishly.

Active means there is a choice. Often there is a clear intention on the part of the anorexic to create pain for the spouse as a byproduct of making him or herself safe, distant, or in control. Active means each act of withholding intimacy from the spouse is an act for which the anorexic is responsible, and can change with recovery.

Withholding: This part of the definition is quite simple. I have something, but I won't give it to you. An intimacy anorexic has intimacy, but he gives it to friends and colleagues and simply withholds it from his spouse.

I have heard hundreds of spouses complain about how the anorexic seems to give intimacy to strangers and friends regularly. It is when they close the door to the world and they are alone that the anorexic's heart closes and he intentionally withholds what he freely gives to others.

Emotions: Emotional intimacy says to the spouse, "Here is my heart, flaws and all. I open it as much as I can, and behold your heart as well."

Everyone in the real world of relationships knows that pain is part of the relationship process. Emotional intimacy does not say, "I connect, give myself and receive you, _if_ you promise never to hurt me, see or mention my flaws, or disagree with me." This conditional intimacy and irrational need for safety in intimacy anorexics is very common. Withholding emotional intimacy says that regardless of how much of my heart I can access and give to you, I will not share my emotional or authentic self with you. This is a choice.

Spiritual: The spiritual part of a human being is by far the most intimate part. Our spirit is not only the universal place that wants to connect with God, but our spirit is a place of knowing, discerning, and having intuition or a sense of things that goes beyond facts.

Spirituality with our spouses is one of the most sacred things on earth. Regardless of the manifestation of worship, prayer, meditation or other connecting rituals, when we share this inner person with our spouses, we share our authentic self more purely than mere words can express.

The intimacy anorexic says, "No! I'm not letting you into that sacred place." The religious intimacy anorexic will pray with others, but will rarely pray, worship, or open her spirit up to her spouse. Not allowing the spouse in spiritually is intentional. Again, regardless of skill or background, we all have a spirit. Giving the spiritual part of ourselves to our spouse is an important ingredient for intimacy in marriage.

Sexual: Sexual intimacy can be electrifyingly intimate inside a marriage when both spouses are giving and receiving within the sexual encounter. Just as we are emotional and spiritual, we are all sexual. We were sexual from the first slap on the behind at birth and will be until our last breath.

Sexuality is far more than an act; it is part of who we are. Intimacy anorexics can either deny they are sexual or engage as little of themselves as possible in the act of sexuality. The majority of anorexics, male and female, do not mind the act of sex. It is the giving of their heart or connecting during sex that is scary. The anorexic would say that he will give you his body but not his soul or spirit during sex.

This one-dimensional sex (physical sex), over time, can become unsatisfying for the spouse, or even an unattractive proposition altogether. Some anorexics purposely negatively reinforce sex so their spouses will not want to be sexual with them.

Another smaller number of intimacy anorexics will have nothing to do with sex. They avoid sex in so many ways by shutting themselves down and, over time, starve or punish their spouses with the lack of sex, intentionally creating a sexless marriage at the cost of their spouses' happiness. This desire to be unknown is intentional. It says, "I will not let you in, no way, no way, no matter what pain I intentionally inflict on you. Too bad for you."

Withholding or sabotaging sex is a part of the intimacy anorexia pattern for some; a primary part for others. However, it is a very small part of the intimacy anorexia pattern for some.

Intimacy: Intimacy is the ability for me to let you behold me, flaws and all. I have heard some say intimacy is in-to-me-see. That's clever, and I think you get the point. The intimacy anorexic prefers to be regarded as altogether good. Prior to recovery, the intimacy anorexic has great difficulty letting her spouse see her flawed self.

Interestingly, as intimacy anorexia progresses in a soul, over time, she becomes less able to see the positives in her spouse. It is as if she becomes all the good of humanity and her spouse becomes all the bad. It is difficult to be intimate if one spouse is good and the other is bad.

Intimacy means I am flawed and loved and you are flawed and loved. I let you see me, and you let me see you. For most intimacy anorexics, the only answer to an invitation to intimacy is no.

Intimacy can be scary for anyone, regardless of gender. For the intimacy anorexic, intimacy can be terrifying beyond belief. Interestingly enough, intimacy is the only solution for an intimacy anorexic.

Spouse: As mentioned earlier, there is something about marriage that demands what the anorexic wants to withhold, and that is long-term emotional, spiritual, and sexual intimacy. Even a marriage between healthy people can be challenging at times.

Inside a marriage, we all experience pain, rejection, anger, disappointment, and the whole gamut of emotions. If you are an intimacy anorexic, you recoil from this type of pain within a relationship. Then the dance of anorexia begins. The anorexic recoils or pushes the spouse away and the spouse has to create ways of dealing with this rejection, trying to get intimacy from someone who is actively withholding it.

The anorexic applies a variety of strategies to create and maintain distance in the relationship. This distance allows the intimacy anorexic to feel safe, protected, and in control. The intimacy anorexic is not going to allow him or herself to be threatened by genuine intimacy. The strategies anorexics use effectively to create distance differ from couple to couple. However, over time, you can see anorexic strategies build a fortress against their spouses.

The spouse really is the primary target of the addict. Others will be impacted either directly or indirectly by this addiction to withholding; however, the person with the most consequences from intimacy anorexia is the spouse.

I have seen amazing courage displayed by both intimacy anorexics and their spouses. The spouse can even be a man or woman who has written a huge check to keep the marriage together, despite the blame and vilification he or she has endured over the years. When intimacy anorexia has been clearly identified, and the anorexic accepts full responsibility for the withholding behaviors, both of their lives can be changed dramatically.

Love and intimacy are possible. I have seen changed people and changed marriages over the decades. I have seen miracles of recovery from many addiction processes, including intimacy anorexia.

The intimacy anorexic who chooses recovery can positively affect his own life and the lives of those he loves. So, keep reading. Regardless of the past damage done by the intimacy anorexic, if there is effort and willingness in his soul, recovery can happen.

Characteristics

Now that we have defined intimacy anorexia somewhat, we are at a point where we need to be even more specific about what we are discussing. So far, you have heard me use the term *withholding* as it relates to intimacy anorexia. Now I want to discuss the particular behaviors indicative of intimacy anorexia.

To eye these behaviors independently—here and there or observe only a few—will not give you the ability to understand intimacy anorexia. This is what is so helpful about having a clear paradigm. With a clear paradigm, you will be able to piece A, B, and C together as an end product and live life accordingly. This can be no truer than with the paradigm of intimacy anorexia. Here I lay out ten specific characteristics of intimacy anorexia. I will also throw in an extra one I often hear from my clients or their spouses.

As you read through this chapter, if you are the anorexic, try to keep your heart and mind open. If you are not sure if a characteristic applies to you, ask your spouse. He or she will most likely be able to give you a clear picture, from their perspective. As in any list of characteristics, you won't necessarily display all ten, but you or your spouse may have enough characteristics to still qualify for being an intimacy anorexic.

Busy

The first characteristic of an intimacy anorexic is *being so busy you have little time for the spouse.* This is a very common characteristic of most intimacy anorexics. This does not necessarily mean the spouse travels all the time, though that could definitely be a way to avoid intimacy. Busyness can include anything from productive activities, volunteering, reading, computer time, or anything else that justifies why the intimacy anorexic cannot be with his or her spouse in a quality manner.

"Busy" takes so many forms, it could be a book all by itself. Any of these behaviors could be fine in a marriage if she, the anorexic, stayed connected to her spouse. In the absence of connecting, "busy" becomes a way for the intimacy anorexic to actually withhold intimacy—even the potential for intimacy—through avoidance.

Blame

Blame, as an anorexic characteristic, is almost universal. *When an issue or problem comes up in the marriage; the anorexic blames or puts responsibility on the spouse for it before he can see his contribution to the problem or issue.* As you understand anorexia better and how an intimacy anorexic wants to be in the "good box" all the time, it makes being flawed, irresponsible, thoughtless, careless, and bad less desirable to discuss (if you are the anorexic).

Blaming is almost reflexive for many anorexics. I am absolutely amazed at how much the emotional survival of the anorexic is at stake if he is found to be flawed like the rest of us. Often he cannot be honest about his intentional withholding. Starving his spouse directly affects the behavior he receives back from his spouse.

Withholding Love

The anorexic often has a difficult time perceiving the intangible nature of withholding love. To withhold love is *to not give to your spouse love the way you know to or how they have asked to be loved.* Each one of us wants to be loved, and yet we all experience being loved in many different ways. Spouses may want emotional sharing, long walks, or a thoughtful note or gift that says, "I was thinking of you." Some just want help around the house or with the children. However, the spouse needs to be shown love, and the anorexic already knows how the spouse wants to be loved.

Here is how to know what type of love your spouse needs, and if you are withholding it from him or her. The anorexic convinces her future spouse that she loves him in the way she receives love. This leads him to the decision to marry her. Think back to when you dated your spouse. First, what meant a lot to him or her? Second, when you really get in trouble in your marriage—or the marriage is threatened—what do you do to make up or show you care? Finally, if your life was dependent upon your answer, could you say you know how your spouse feels your love the most? If you are the intimacy anorexic, and you agree now that you know how your spouse receives love, then why is he doing without it? If you do not have a clear, rational reason without blaming, then let me suggest you are actively, intentionally withholding love from your spouse.

Withholding Praise

The withholding of praise is also a significantly recurring behavior for intimacy anorexics. To withhold praise is *to not share with your spouse her positive qualities and her positive impact on your life.* Let's go back to, "as if your life was dependent upon your answer..." If you had to write ten things that are amazing and positive about your spouse, or how he or she is impacting your life in a positive way, my bet is, again, you could absolutely make a list pretty quickly.

If you are an anorexic, think about the last week or month and how frequently you intentionally praised your spouse. How often are you praising your spouse in front of their family, your friends, or even your children? If you are the spouse of an anorexic, reflect on this as well. When was the last time you really received heartfelt praise without asking for it from your spouse?

All of us have amazing positive qualities. Anorexia, over time, closes this positive vision and tends to create focus on the flaws of the spouse.

If you have not been praising your spouse regularly for who he is and all he does, may I suggest that you could be actively and intentionally not praising him?

Withholding Sex

By far, of all the behaviors that are characteristics of intimacy anorexics, withholding sex is probably the easiest to measure, and at the very least, most obvious. *Withholding sex from your spouse is avoiding having sex, sabotaging sexual encounters, or not connecting emotionally during sex.* You can tell whether you are the spouse or the anorexic by analyzing the last time you had sex. It might not be as easy for the anorexic to remember the last time he or she sabotaged a sexual encounter, or whether it was before, during, or after the encounter. It is even harder for the anorexic to remember withholding emotionally and spiritually during sex, or really giving all of him or herself. Any of these behaviors can be a way of withholding sex. In the intimacy anorexia workbook, I give some of these examples:

- During sex, do you look at your spouse or close your eyes?
- Do you think of other things to do during sex?
- Do you fantasize about others or porn during sex?
- Do you communicate positively during sex?
- Are you silent during sex?
- Do you act as if you dread sex?
- Do you hurry your spouse to get it over with?
- Do you leave your spouse emotionally or physically after sex?
- Do you shut your spouse down when talking about sex?

Withholding Spiritually

The spouse might not notice the withholding of spirituality. Some of my clients have been spiritual leaders, pastors, rabbis, and even medicine men who did not connect with their spouses spiritually. Withholding spiritually is *withholding spiritual connectedness from your spouse*. This means, regardless of faith practices or the lack thereof, there exists no real spiritually connective behavior with the spouse. The anorexic might be religious to the hilt, but not spiritually authentic in the presence of her spouse.

I have heard countless excuses, especially from the religious anorexic (regardless of faith). *I do this just by myself. It's not my personality. My spouse is too spiritual (or not spiritual enough), so I do not connect with her spiritually.* Regardless of the rationalization, there is an absence of spiritual connection between the intimacy anorexic and her spouse.

Feelings

This characteristic can be described as *being unwilling or unable to share feelings with one's spouse.* Having difficulty sharing feelings is also a universal characteristic of the intimacy anorexic. As stated earlier, addictions hinder emotional development.

If you are the spouse of an intimacy anorexic, you may have difficulty remembering a time when your husband or wife voluntarily shared feelings with you without having to write the "emotional check" for the experience. If the anorexic's image of the marriage is threatened or he or she really blows it somehow, you can expect them to share some feelings, but that positive behavior fades away within a week or two after the activating event.

Sharing one's feelings is an act of authenticity that can be scary and difficult for intimacy anorexics. Their unwillingness or inability to share feelings can be intentional, so as not to give you love the way they know you like it. There is a time when this could legitimately be due to a skill deficit. In that case, when he or she does the Emotional Communication Exercise with you, you will both experience real effort at connecting. While doing the Feeling Exercise, if the anorexic is not trying to connect, but appears to be checking off a box indicating otherwise, you will experience the "unwilling" part of this addiction to withholding.

Criticism

Ongoing or ungrounded criticism which leads to distance in the marriage is the seventh characteristic of intimacy anorexia. This can consist of low-grade put-downs toward the spouse, noticing what she does wrong, or just regularly pointing out that her ideas are bad.

The ungrounded criticism has little to do with reality. The strategy might be to push the spouse away or throw her off the trail of something. Either way, it intentionally creates distance.

This sort of criticism does not need to be spoken to be felt. So many spouses have told me that their husband or wife does not actually speak critically, but they can still feel it constantly.

If criticism is an active strategy, the intimacy anorexic will be much faster at making a list of what is wrong, defective, or weak about his spouse than about what is amazing. The anorexic could also employ criticism as a binge tactic to push the other away at times when intimacy or sex might be expected or on birthdays, holidays, or right before vacations.

This is the intimacy anorexic pushing the spouse away so he does not have to emotionally or sexually give to the spouse.

Anger/Silence

Not all intimacy anorexics use silence or anger characteristically. However, those that use anger or silence use it with a vengeance. This intimacy anorexia characteristic can be described as *any use of anger or silence to push away, punish, or control the spouse.*

I have logged countless hours listening to stories from spouses and intimacy anorexics alike about the employment of anger or silence toward the spouse. Sometimes the examples are extreme, including times when the intimacy anorexic will not talk to her spouse for days or weeks while living in the same house. The anger explosion is often over something minor, and is a great tool to push the spouse away to avoid giving her heart to him.

If the intimacy anorexic uses anger or silence as a tool, you can expect it often. If the intimacy anorexic chooses recovery, conquering this behavior will require consequences and boundaries. This characteristic is best explained by real-life examples such as those listed below from intimacy anorexics and their spouses.

Money

The characteristic of *controlling or shaming the spouse about money issues* is probably the least common among intimacy anorexics. Those who employ it do so with an iron fist. Most of the anorexics who control or shame with money do so by keeping the spouse ignorant of the finances, giving the spouse an allowance, making the spouse ask for money, and refusing to allow the spouse to have a credit card or checkbook.

However, there is the other side of controlling through money as well. I call it controlling through abundance. This spouse has substantial money, but controls with it. The spouse's attitude is as follows: I buy you everything, so do not complain about a lack of intimacy, love, or sex. This type of control through money is not as obvious as control through not giving.

Shaming the spouse about money can also be a part of this intimacy anorexic characteristic. In this case, it is perfectly okay for the intimacy anorexic to spend money on anything he or she desires, but the spouse has to account for everything, or is put down for purchases, even legitimate ones.

Free

Remember at the beginning of the chapter I said I would throw in a free characteristic. Well, here it is. The keyword would be "roommate." *The spouse of the anorexic feels like merely a roommate.* I have heard this same comment so many times from spouses that I oftentimes add it to the end of my assessment for determining the diagnosis for anorexia.

Congratulations, you have gathered a lot of information regarding intimacy anorexia. Below I have listed the ten characteristics again. There are three ways to respond. I list each characteristic along with a place to respond with "Y" (Yes) or "N" (No). First, respond as you see your behavior. Second, respond as your spouse might see your behavior (assuming you are the anorexic). Third, provide your spouse's actual response.

Characteristic	As I'd Respond	As I think Spouse Would Respond	My Spouse's Response
Busy	Y N	Y N	Y N
Blame	Y N	Y N	Y N
Withholding Love	Y N	Y N	Y N
Withholding Praise	Y N	Y N	Y N
Withholding Sex	Y N	Y N	Y N
Withholding Spirituality	Y N	Y N	Y N
Feelings	Y N	Y N	Y N
Criticism	Y N	Y N	Y N
Anger/Silence	Y N	Y N	Y N
Money	Y N	Y N	Y N

If you or your spouse has five or more Yes responses to these characteristics, I would encourage you to keep reading; you are most likely an intimacy anorexic. If you have many more than five Yes responses, then you definitely have this roadblock that can limit your emotional fitness. I would encourage you to get more information on intimacy anorexia at www.intimacyanorexia.com. Remember, there is always hope for those who are willing and able to apply the effort to change.

If intimacy anorexia sounds like something you are dealing with, I recommend you also purchase the book or DVD, *Intimacy Anorexia* (Discovery Press) along with the workbooks. If you are married to someone with intimacy anorexia, I recommend the book, DVD, and workbooks *Married and Alone* (Discovery Press) for yourself.

Intimacy anorexia is a very challenging issue. In most cases, you will need professional help and support groups. I highly recommend a 3 or 5-day Intimacy Anorexia Intensive in my office to jump start your recovery.

Whether you have an addiction, intimacy anorexia, or both issues, you can pursue emotional fitness. Pursuing emotional fitness will enhance any recovery process you may find yourself in. My hope is that whatever steps you need to take for your health, you take them.

Unclogging

In earlier chapters, you began work on the building blocks of emotional fitness by identifying and communicating your emotions. I hope you are being consistent with your emotional identification and communication as you continue reading. This chapter is going to give you insight into why you may be emotionally underdeveloped or even stunted.

This chapter may be the most important to help you unclog the negative emotional effects of past events. Once you are able to unclog, you will find new freedom to feel and be present with your emotions.

I recently had the pleasure of meeting one of the nicest ladies I have ever met. Tina came to see me because her marriage lacked sex. Her husband suffered from intimacy anorexia: the active withholding of spiritual, emotional, and sexual intimacy from his spouse. Tina was a big-hearted woman who has gone to the same Baptist church for more than a decade. While talking with Tina, I uncovered that as a child, both her mother and father were extremely neglectful and at times emotionally abusive. I helped Tina work through the unclogging exercise, and I watched how her emotional fitness accelerated tremendously as a result.

Andrew, like many men, came to see me for help in his struggle with pornography. Addiction to pornography can set one's emotional development back to the age when the addiction became consistently active. On top of that, we uncovered another factor causing Andrew's emotional underdevelopment. His mother was emotionally and physically abusive. This abuse left him so clogged that he would physically constrict his body anytime he went to her home for a visit. It began in the car as he traveled and lasted the entire length of the visit. I had Andrew work through the unclogging exercise. Not only did

Andrew accelerate his emotional fitness; he was also able to visit his mother without any constriction in his body or emotions.

We all have stories. Neglect, abuse, or trauma can hurt deeply, and can cause people to shut down emotionally. Before we look into the unclogging exercise, I want to review the ways in which people experience abuse, neglect, or trauma. Many who have been emotionally unfit have visited the various emotions—I like to call them "cities"—of abandonment, abuse or neglect. This excerpt is from the book *Get a Grip: How to Take Control of the Things That Are Controlling You* (Siloam, 2006).

Abandonment

The city of abandonment is often cold and windy. Abandonment comes in many different forms. I will do my best to visit several of the neighborhoods of abandonment.

The downtown of abandonment is called total abandonment. Total abandonment can be a willful abandonment or a non-willful abandonment by a parent. Willful abandonment could have happened when you were born illegitimately and one or both of your parents abandoned you. This willful abandonment might have happened for various reasons. If you were adopted, you would have definitely visited the downtown of total abandonment. If your parents sent you to live in foster homes, with relatives, or sent you to boarding schools, these too are forms of willful abandonment.

These types of abandonments are intentional actions by one or both of your parents. The intentions of some of them were totally selfish: They did not want you. They wanted to live their own lives or chase their own dreams, lovers, or careers. Some parents' motives may have been to give you a chance at a better life. Still, the abandonment of the total self is a city of origin for influences toward what may have control over you.

The neighborhoods around downtown break up into several suburbs. Each suburb represents a part of you abandoned or neglected by one or both parents. We will make short trips into these neighborhoods since you may have been to at least one before.

The abandonment of your spirit is our first suburb to visit in the town of abandonment. If one or both of your parents abandoned you spiritually, you would not have received any spiritual training or the encouragement needed to develop the spiritual aspects of yourself as a child.

Spiritual abandonment feels as if your parents decided you did not have a spirit, so they spent very little or no time communicating about spiritual matters with you. Your contact with a community of faith would have been totally nonexistent. Another form of spiritual abandonment would have been if one or both of your parents were so rigidly religious that you were not allowed to explore honest questions of a spiritual nature.

The next abandonment you may have experienced is abandonment of your emotions. Emotional abandonment is a confusing area of town. It is as if the city engineers forgot to put names on the streets. You travel down a road, and you do not know the name of it nor how to get to another street you do not know.

In the United States, one or both parents may have emotionally abandoned their children. I do not think it was intentional. I do not think your mom and dad had a business meeting and said, "Hey, let's abandon our children's feelings." Remember, more than likely, your parent's feelings were abandoned as well. They were probably raised under the bad idea that, "Children are to be seen and not heard."

Such a parent might also have raised you. In your family, several things happen to the emotional part of your being when it is abandoned. You learn that feelings are not valid at all; you are typically taught that you are not to identify, trust, or feel a feeling. If you are feeling full you cannot listen to your body communicate the full feeling; you will still "have to eat what is on your plate."

You cannot cry if you feel like crying since "big boys don't cry." You receive so many mixed messages that your emotional self is not vocal, not trustworthy, or not important. In turn, you then have very little training about how to identify or communicate your feelings. You will also gain little training on how to utilize feelings in a decision-making process. This can lead you to stay totally in your head or to be so emotionally based in your decisions that you keep making more bad ones.

You will likely not learn what it is like to be emotionally honest and available in an intimate relationship. I think you can see how visiting the suburb of emotional abandonment as a child can definitely be a genesis for the influence of out of control behavior.

Abandonment of your gifting is another stop on this tour. This suburb is confusing as well. It is like you are in a part of town that speaks a different language and has a different currency than you. One or both of your parents have not investigated your particular gifts. They may not have allowed you to experiment with various sports, music, or art in order to see what your natural aptitude might have been.

Another form of abandonment would be their refusal to allow you to develop a gift they knew you had. You may have been athletic, musically inclined, just liked to fix things, or asked a lot of questions. Your parents would not allow you to develop a gift they actually knew you possessed. This lack of accepting and nurturing your giftedness can definitely be a genesis for out of control behavior.

The abandonment of affection is familiar to many trying to gain control over their lives. All babies come with a built-in need (not a desire) to be touched and hugged. This need for affection remains until death. The abandonment of affection starves the soul who experiences this. You are confused because your body really wants a hug, cuddle, and pat on the back, and yet it is as if mom, dad, or both do not see that your body needs touch. The abandonment of affection is definitely a place for an influence of behaviors that can get control over you.

Financial abandonment has two neighborhoods. The very rich live somewhere on the north side and the poor, in debt, and struggling to live, on the south side. The interesting thing about this town is there are no roads to travel on. Nobody knows how to get to one another's place, and it seems as if it is all guesswork.

If you were financially abandoned, you probably know exactly what I mean—you may not understand finances at all. Nobody taught you about saving, investing, and how money actually works. Often you were exposed to either the "work/spend existence" model or the "mystery" model of money.

You feel inadequate, even if you earn well. Again, parents who neglect the financial aspects of their children rarely do this intentionally. I find that financial abandonment can continue way on up a family tree. This financial abandonment can most definitely be an influence in controlling behavior.

Sexual abandonment is very common in our culture as well. Cities are filled with billboards everywhere urging you to exchange sexuality for something, whether "love" or simply a good time, without mentioning the consequences of pregnancy, disease, shame, and a whole lot more.

Sexual abandonment also tends to run down a family tree. In some families it is as if you are not really sexual. You get either no message at all or confusing things like, "Sex is bad, nasty, and save it for the one you love," as one client told me her parents insinuated.

Being sexual is part of being human. Being sexual is part of who we are and always will be as part of who we are, until death.

Managing sexuality without clarity from one's parents is difficult. The culture attempts to steal sex from its adolescents. Sexual abandonment is so common that I have seen control evolve from it. The roots for out of control behavior stemming from sexual abandonment can be some of the strongest roots of all.

The suburb of moral abandonment is a smoggy city. Things are not real clear here. The smog is not anyone's fault; it just is. Morality tells us what is absolutely right and absolutely wrong, and it is imperative to navigate life with as few crashes as possible.

Morality has been given a bad rap in a culture that wants us to be led by our feelings so others can manipulate us. Parents can avoid this by being real clear with right and wrong for various reasons. Some parents fear being misunderstood or judged by others. Some parents are unclear on moralities, even the basics, due to issues in their own life: lying, stealing, infidelity, and more. Regardless of the reason for moral abandonment, it is a bastion for influences that can later get control of your life.

This town of abandonment is a big city with many suburbs. Some of us have lived in just one part of town. Some of us have been moved from one part of town to another part of town during our developing years. Regardless of the city of abandonment you have lived in, the following chapters can help you break your ties to them so you can live where there is acceptance, love, and peace.

Now that you have taken the tour, take a moment to reflect on your own journey as a child and in adolescence. Did you visit or live in any of the suburbs of abandonment? Below is a list of the abandonments we already mentioned. You can check off any boxes that you feel apply to you. If you are thinking about someone else to whom these might apply, you can take a separate sheet of paper and fill it in based upon your limited knowledge of the abandonment experiences they might have had. Finally, mark the abandonment that applies to you:

Total Abandonment   _____

Spiritual Abandonment   _____

Emotional Abandonment   _____

Gifting Abandonment   _____

Affection Abandonment   _____

Financial Abandonment   _____

Sexual Abandonment   _____

Moral Abandonment   _____

Abuse

Abuse is the intentional violation of another person's spirit, soul, or body, including their emotions or their sexuality. Abuse damages the soul of a developing person on so many levels. Abuse is like taking a Colt .44 and blasting it into a computer. There is no telling exactly how it will damage the computer. The same is true of the effects of abuse on people. For some, abuse damages memories and self-esteem and causes posttraumatic stress and addiction. It also affects the choices the abused person makes and causes all kinds of dysfunction.

Physical abuse is usually one of the easier abuses to identify by someone who has experienced it. Physical abuse is when one or both of your parents, siblings, neighbors, schoolmates, or a stranger has physically hit you, and you knew you were hit. You might have been hit repeatedly or on a number of occasions. If the abuse came from a parent, there could potentially have been years of abuse. Physical abuse can also include demanded physical tasks that were cruel or way beyond your developmental capabilities.

Emotional abuse is common among those who are trying to become emotionally fit. Children who experienced this growing up had parents or other people of influence who would yell at them or shame them. They may have enmeshed you as a surrogate adult in the family. Often you were shamed just for being a child or for being yourself. This chaos and unpredictability can definitely be an influence in a soul's life.

Spiritual abuse is a little trickier to detect than emotional or physical abuse. A religious (not necessarily spiritual) person who is significant to the child demands total compliance with a religious belief. This person is shaming, controlling, and often so rigid that it is difficult to be in relationship with him or her. Being right is more important than love in this spiritual relationship.

The effects of spiritual abuse vary from person to person. Some feel confused. Some question their own spiritual development. Others forfeit all spirituality for fear of being controlled by others. Spiritual abuse can be a festering ground for influences that drive future out of control behaviors.

Sexual abuse is one of the most damaging of the abuses one can experience. The sexual shame often attached to this experience, whether one time or multiple times, is overwhelming for a child, teen, or adult.

Sexual abuse is often kept secret and poorly received when finally disclosed, which can lead to even more problems for survivors of sexual abuse. The repercussions of sexual abuse, especially if the abuse continues to be a secret, are multidirectional. The influence of this abuse is often an anchoring for future out of control behavior.

In regard to all the forms of abuse you may have experienced, you certainly did not choose them, nor did you deserve them, and yet you have to deal with many of the consequences of them. I liken this to a person walking downtown on a sunny afternoon and being struck by a bullet unexpectedly. The person did not ask to be shot and did not deserve to be shot. The pain management and physical therapy to restore movement (if movement has been impaired) is now the victim's responsibility.

Acknowledging the abuses that have occurred in your life can be a huge hurdle to get over. Many sexual abuse survivors tend to beat themselves up about what they wish they had done. They often come up against their own denial of abusive events so as not to shatter the image of themselves they made to protect themselves. They may also have fear about being honest regarding the abuse. I know several clients who felt if they were honest about their abuse they would devolve uncontrollably and never be sane again. It may sound irrational, but when you are afraid, being rational is not a requirement.

Place a check next to the abuses listed below that you feel you experienced as a child.

Physical Abuse   _____

Emotional Abuse   _____

Spiritual Abuse   _____

Sexual Abuse   _____

Sexual Shame

Some of you who are trying to become emotionally fit may have sexual shame. Most of us have done things sexually that we are not proud of. For some, this shame includes years of viewing pornography and masturbation. For others, it is the one time they had premarital sex or a homosexual encounter they never told anyone about.

For others, the sexual shame of affairs or other sexual behaviors they participated in plagues their conscience. Sexual shame is attached to very specific events. These memories often haunt individuals for decades. Your secrets, especially sexual secrets, can definitely be a breeding ground for influences for future self-sabotage.

Sexual shame is often the hardest to overcome. I will not recommend that you write these behaviors in this book. It is important, however, for you to be honest with yourself. On a separate sheet of paper, write out in very direct statements to which your sexual shame is attached.

Once you write down these statements, you should destroy the paper. You can burn it, shred it, or black out all the text; however, you want to destroy it. There is no need to have a permanent record of your sexual shame. However, there is a need for you to be honest with yourself about it.

In the space below, just enter the date on which you wrote out your sexual shame list: The date I wrote down my sexually shameful events was _____, 20____.

Abortions

Here is the king of secrets. For both men and women, aborting a child is probably one of the darkest acts in which they have ever participated. Tens of millions of abortions have been carried out in our culture, which means twice as many as this number have participated in them.

Obviously, the person most impacted by this event is the woman whose baby was aborted. In counseling women for almost two decades, I can tell you that women who have participated in an abortion have huge issues related to the experience.

Witnessing the gut-wrenching tears flowing from the eyes of women of all ages, races, and religions tells me the resultant pain, shame, fear, and self-loathing are universal. Regardless of the pressure she may have faced from others to abort, abortion is a huge contributor to emotional clogging.

Abortion, however, does not just impact the woman; it also impacts the man whose baby is aborted. I have counseled many men over the years who had to work through their issues surrounding an abortion, and it was deeply emotional and life-changing for them. For the man, the secrecy and shame of participating in an abortion also caused them to stay emotionally clogged.

Abortion, similar to sexual shame, is not something I would have you write down in this book. On a separate sheet of paper, write down the issues pertaining to the abortion in which you participated. If you have no issues pertaining to abortions, you can just note below that you read this section and are just checking off that you read it. If you participated in an abortion, use your checkoff as a point of accountability.

_____ I read this section and did what applied to me.

You may identify with one or several areas of abuse, neglect, or trauma. These may have happened to you within family relationships. You may have experienced these issues in a dating relationship or marriage. You may have been abused, raped, or otherwise injured by a stranger. Regardless of how you received the wounds of neglect, abandonment, or abuse, they are now yours and you can take 100 percent responsibility to gain healing and unclog the issues in your life and soul.

First Step

I realize some of you did not experience abandonment, abuse, or neglect growing up; however, as we have talked through them, some forgotten memories from the past may have surfaced.

The first step in unclogging is to be honest with yourself about those who have caused you pain. The people who have hurt you may have done so intentionally or unintentionally. However, regardless of intentionality, the pain you experienced was (or is) still real for you.

I want you to take a sheet of paper and write down the names of people who have hurt you. After you make a list of names, write out in a sentence or two the pain they have caused in your life. Finally, rank the listed items from least painful to most painful. I realize each situation is painful, but ranking them will get you ready to do the rest of the unclogging exercise.

1. Make a list

2. Write a short statement

3. Rank

Unclog Exercise

If you have any health issues, please see a physician for permission to do this exercise.

The Anger Letter

The next step in the unclogging exercise is to choose someone on your list of people who has hurt you and write an anger letter to him or her (a letter you will never send). I recommend you start with the person who has caused you the least pain. However, if your intuition is directing you to a specific person, it is good to write him or her a letter as well. I often tell my clients to imagine this person in the room and unable to talk or move. You can say whatever you need to him or her in this letter. This is not a letter to suppress but rather to let out all the thoughts and feelings of hate, disgust, anger, confusion, and anguish that have impacted your soul. This letter is not an "I forgive you" letter. That will come later. This is an opportunity for you to rid yourself of the anger that has been a part of your soul. These wounds, if not addressed, make becoming emotionally fit more difficult. A wounded person acts a lot differently in a relationship than someone who is healthy or more healed. I know this from experience. The purpose of this step is to simply express your anger in letter form toward the person who caused you pain.

Warm Up

For this part of the exercise, you will need something to hit and something to hit with (a padded baseball bat or tennis racket work well). First, warm up your body. Then take your bat and hit your mattress or pillow first with light blows, then medium, heavy, and extra heavy wallops. I recommend you do this three consecutive times. Then warm up your voice as well. Using the word "No" along with the hits, do soft, medium, loud, and extra loud No's with your voice while hitting. This may feel awkward, but removing this buildup of pain from your soul and spirit feels almost like having a baby, so you want to be physically warmed-up.

While you are warming up, you may want to make sure you are home alone. I would also recommend disconnecting the phone so you are not disturbed.

Read the Letter Out Loud

After your physical warm-up, take the letter you wrote to this person and read it out loud. If the person's name is Toby, then you would read the letter out loud like this: "Toby, how could you have done this to me? I trusted you!..."

Of course Toby is nowhere around. You certainly do not need to do this with him or her around. You are simply in a room alone, reading the letter aloud.

Engage the Anger Physically and Verbally

After reading your letter, put it down and pick up your bat. You can hit the bed or pillow and let Toby have it, symbolically. You can yell, scream, or cry, but let the infection out that has been robbing you. You can symbolically tell Toby, "Your secrets are not controlling me anymore and you are to blame!" You have no limit as to what you can say to this person. For once, let go of all the control that is keeping your wound infected. Let it out!

This can last anywhere from fifteen minutes to an hour. Usually your body will let you know when you are done spiritually, emotionally, and physically, and finished putting this behind you.

You are worth getting it all out and finding healing. Someone has given you something toxic. You have been unhealthy ever since. After you remove it from you, you will feel so much better.

Comments

When you do the unclogging exercise, you should only work on one person on your list at a time. If you have been injured by three different people, it will require three different unclogging exercises. DO NOT do this exercise once for all the different people who have hurt you. Each "bullet" needs to be removed separately.

Each person you do an unclogging exercise for may give you a different experience or even insight. Some men and women who do this think the person at the top of their list is going to be the worst, but find that someone down the list a bit produced a much larger, more painful experience for them to work through.

In my personal and professional experience I can attest that unclogging can be truly life-changing. I cannot tell you how many clients of mine have watched this technique on one of my DVDs and waited to do it until they came to my office during an intensive. In my office, I have watched people use this exercise to physical depletion, but by the next day, they felt much better and their eyes were even brighter.

My encouragement is for you to actually take the time and do this exercise. Do not just read it; have a plan to unclog and see how it impacts you. Those who do this exercise take a huge step toward emotional fitness.

Unchaining

We all know the familiar experience of watching a movie surrounded by family or friends with the aroma of popcorn in the air. Think about the last superhero movie you watched. Inevitably, the nemesis of the superhero lures him into a situation where the superhero becomes trapped and chained up in some way. The tension builds and you wonder if the hero will actually be able to free him or herself.

Then it happens. The sidekick shows up; an internal struggle commences. The nemesis makes a mistake, and the superhero engages a power to snap himself out of the chains. He is back on his mission to save the world and defeat his nemesis.

Most of us identify with the trapped superhero. You were designed to live happier and more fulfilled than you may be currently. You may even feel chained. This chapter deals with how to be set free and unchained.

In the last chapter, we explored several ways your soul might have been damaged or chained. Hopefully you have already done the unclogging exercise enough to feel that proverbial snap of chains that held you. When I did the unclogging exercise, it was a life changer for me. My soul felt free, and the range of emotions I felt I could not even put into words at the time.

However, like the superhero removing the chains, this is only the first part of the process. There is still more for us to get free from. This next process can literally unchain you from the people in your past who have intentionally and unintentionally caused pain in your life. The process is very powerful, but <u>only</u> do it after you have done the unclogging exercise.

Many clients have come into my office having done a version of this next exercise without doing the unclogging exercise first. The results left them walking around wounded, thinking they had already dealt with the issue.

If you are having a significant reaction now to an event from the past, that event is most likely not healed. If you find yourself overreacting to a person or event that is similar to the earlier abuse, neglect, or trauma, you probably still need healing.

Craig was an executive who had been married to his wife Sam for more than thirty years. Their marriage was in really bad shape when they showed up in my office for an intensive. In the first session, I always have each spouse describe their perspective of what is going on in the marriage and the salient issues so I can assess the marital structures. Craig described his perspective of the marital issues first. When it was Sam's turn, within a minute of her starting to share, Craig interrupted her, yelling, "You're not going to control me. Nobody tells me what to do!"

Craig's reaction was way out of proportion to what Sam was sharing. As I learned more about Craig, I found out his mom was a control freak— on steroids. She did not let him speak, feel, or do hardly anything without controlling it. I had him do the unclogging exercise and he experienced great relief. Then I had him do the unchaining exercise. Afterwards, he was able to break away from his past and reengage his wife in the present without reacting to a simple request. Craig was unchained and the result was a better marriage for both of them.

Cindy was a single, young executive climbing the corporate ladder. She had a series of short-term relationships, but ended them before she became emotionally intimate. Cindy wanted to change her pattern because she felt the man she was dating was the man of her dreams. She realized the pattern and did not want to push him away. However, Cindy had a secret she had not shared with anyone prior to coming to counseling.

When Cindy was sixteen, a popular senior asked her to the prom. She was excited about going out with him and picked out the perfect dress. On prom night, he came to get her, but once they were in the car, he told her he wanted to show her something on the way. He took Cindy to a secluded area and raped her, then took her to prom like nothing happened. It was a surreal experience for Cindy. The trauma she endured was extreme. Cindy had never been with anyone sexually before that night. Since then, she has had huge difficulty in trusting men.

When Cindy did the unclogging exercise, she spent thirty minutes letting that rape go. When I came back into the room, Cindy was sweating, but had the biggest smile of relief on her face. The following week, I had her do the unchained exercise and she was able to reclaim her life. She did not marry the guy she came to see me about, but she did get married. Now three children later, she has not once regretted the time she spent unclogging and unchaining so she could live a life of emotional fitness.

Unchaining

Unchaining yourself can be an invaluable experience. It is an exercise and act of your will you do to free yourself from the events and pain of the past.

Unchaining gives you an opportunity to see where you really are in forgiving those who have hurt you. I have done this many times in my life when dealing with my past. I have also done this in current situations that demanded I deal with anger in order to unchain myself.

Before I get to the specifics of the exercise, I want to expose you to some myths about forgiving that I discussed in my book, The 7 Love Agreements (Siloam, 2005).

Myths

1. I must confront my perpetrator to offer him or her forgiveness.

2. My perpetrator must be repentant or broken to be forgiven.

3. My perpetrator must change before I can forgive.

These myths put the very powerful act of forgiveness on the person who caused the pain. That person may not be able to be located or worse, may still not have the maturity to own the darkness they have intentionally or unintentionally released in your life.

The Truth

1. They do not even have to acknowledge, in any way, the pain they caused you so that you can forgive them.

2. They do not have to repent or be broken for you to forgive them.

3. They do not have to change for you to forgive them.

The unclogging exercise removes all the power from the people who hurt you and gives you the power to unchain yourself and release forgiveness back to you. For me, the fact that I had the power to forgive and live, and I did not have to wait for others to do this was a powerful paradigm shift.

You too do not have to wait one more day to truly forgive the people from your past who have legitimately hurt you. As you walk through this exercise, you must simply be authentic. Even if you are unable to forgive at the time of the exercise, it will help you see where you are and that you can try again in the future.

Unchaining Exercise—Step One

Face the two chairs toward each other. Pick a chair and sit facing the other chair. We will call the chair you are sitting in "Chair A."

While you are sitting in Chair A, pretend you are one of the people who has caused you pain. As you role-play this person, have him or her apologize and ask for forgiveness for all he or she did to you.

Then role-play the person as if he or she were mature and fully aware of his or her actions. The perpetrator is hypothetically confessing to you in the other chair, Chair B. If I were doing this exercise about my dad, I would sit in Chair A. I would role-play my dad and verbally own the (his) pain and mistake, and then apologize and ask for forgiveness for the things I did and did not do to Doug in Chair B.

As I play my dad, I might say, "Doug, I need you to forgive me for_____." Now since I am playing my dad, I can say what he needs to in order to own and apologize for the pain he caused me. Start off role-playing this person by saying, "<u>Your name</u>, I need you to forgive me for_____."

Unchaining Exercise—Step Two

I just played my dad as he asked forgiveness of several things, while pretending Doug was in Chair B. I symbolically heard my dad own his mistakes and ask for forgiveness. Now I can start step two, where I sit in Chair B as myself.

After hearing my dad ask for forgiveness, I must decide how I will respond. Above all, I need to be honest. For example, if you are not ready to forgive the person, tell him or her. Perhaps in this case you could promise to try again in a few weeks. Whatever you do when you role-play yourself, do not be fake or do what you think you should do; be real.

If you are able to forgive the person, then tell him or her. As in our example, Doug is now talking to dad who sits in the opposite chair. Doug could say, "Dad, I forgive you." And I, Doug, could really let him go and no longer hold him responsible for his abuses or neglect.

If you are able to forgive this person, it is time to move to step three. If you are not able at this time to forgive the person, get your calendar out and determine a time when you will try this exercise again (shoot for three to four weeks away). Repeat this exercise monthly to measure your progress with anyone you are unable to forgive.

Unchaining—Step Three

In our example, Doug has forgiven Dad. Now I, Doug, stand up from wherever I have been sitting, sit down in Chair A again, and once again play the role of my dad. Doug has just forgiven him. Now it is dad's turn to respond to Doug's forgiveness. Dad (role-played by Doug) might say, "Thanks, Doug," and when dad is done talking to Doug, the exercise is over. So in brief:

Step One—Start in Chair A as the person who caused you pain, who is now asking for forgiveness.

Step Two—Sit in Chair B as yourself, and honestly respond to the person's request for forgiveness.

Step Three—If you have forgiven him or her, go back to Chair A and play this person responding to your forgiveness.

This exercise can be a very emotional one for those with extremely abusive backgrounds, so have a box of tissues ready nearby. Also, make sure you will not be interrupted by the phone or door, etc. It will be important for you to stay focused.

Remember to do this exercise only after you have completed theunchaining exercise. So many people try to forgive before they heal.

Remember that in all these exercises, each person gets individual time in the chair—individual time with you. Again, I do not recommend that you role-play more than two people in a day.

Next Step

If you have done the unchaining exercise for any or all of the people who caused you pain, you have done significant work. Many of my clients report that they feel like the mucus from these events is finally gone from their soul. They report that they feel like the day after having gotten over a cold, when they can finally breathe fully again.

I am excited for you as you work to become the most emotionally fit person you can be. Now I want to take you to another place most people rarely go. Not only have we had others hurt us or make mistakes that caused us pain; we have all "sinned" against our own souls. We may have done things to ourselves that were not bright or well-thought-out and these have caused us pain.

I want you to do the unchaining exercise with yourself. I have watched clients receive tremendous help when they actually take full responsibility for what they have done to themselves or allowed to be done to them in the past. I do not want you to miss the benefits of unchaining yourself.

Start in Chair A as yourself. In Chair B, be the imaginary you. Real Doug sits in Chair A, while Doug is in Chair B. Real Doug owns up, apologizes, and asks forgiveness of imaginary Doug, sitting in Chair B. Real Doug might say, "Doug, I need you to forgive me for..."

Then real Doug stands up and sits in Chair B. I have heard imaginary Doug's request for forgiveness and have responded with forgiveness.

Again, in this exercise, be totally authentic. If you are not able to forgive yourself at this time, it is fine. If such is the case, try again in three or four weeks until you are able to forgive yourself. Self-forgiveness can be a really sweet way to live. We all make mistakes; it is what we do with them that makes a huge difference in how emotionally fit we live our lives.

Last Step

I want to take you to a final step in unchaining yourself from the past. So far you have unchained yourself from those who have caused you pain, and hopefully you have unchained yourself from your past. The next step will bring significant help.

There is one more person you may have hurt; one more person for whom you need to own your past. That person is God. Regardless of your spiritual background or religious training, this exercise can also have profound impact. I encourage you to do this exercise first, before making any judgments and see what the exercise gives you.

In this exercise, you are in Chair A, asking God to forgive you. God is sitting in Chair B. After you complete the exercise asking forgiveness of God, you stand up and sit in Chair B, role-playing how God would respond.

In God's chair, you respond to your request to be forgiven. When God is done talking, stand_up and return to Chair A. Once there, respond to God. I have done this exercise and found it helpful. I have seen thousands do the same and come to feel unchained.

I highly recommend you do all the unchaining exercise to help maximize your ability to be and stay emotionally fit. Below are spaces for you to write the dates when you completed the various unchaining exercises.

I unchained myself from people in my past on _____/_____/_____

I unchained myself from myself on _____/_____/_____

I unchained myself from God on _____/_____/_____

Body Connection

About five years ago I got myself into a situation: I was 15-20 pounds over my ideal weight. I carried this extra weight for a couple years and found it hard to lose.

I applied one of my favorite life principles to my situation: "When you need help, get help." I was connected to a world-class personal trainer through a unique set of circumstances. My goals were to get in shape and lose the weight, and then build muscle. I started working out two or three days a week, depending on my travel schedule. The trainer pushed me beyond what I thought I could do, and over time and with much persistence, I lost the weight and got into really good shape.

I could not wait to tell my trainer when I had lost the weight I wanted to lose. The response I received surprised me.

"Great, now let's get you stronger and bigger like you asked me to do."

I was surprised my trainer remembered my initial goals, but I felt a lack of excitement and celebration from him for all the hard work I had put in.

In light of this, I want to take a few moments to celebrate with you before we continue. If you have been identifying your feelings on a daily basis while reading this book, GOOD JOB! If you have made a list of the people who have caused your pain and have released all that appropriate anger and rage, GREAT! If you really did that hard spirit, soul, and body work, to that effort I say, GOOD JOB! To those who had the courage to unchain themselves from the past, GOOD JOB!

If you are doing the work of becoming emotionally fit, you deserve applause. Not only are you separating yourself from your past, you are preparing yourself to experience a really awesome future. For your family, friends, spouse, and coworkers who will be touched and experience the new emotionally fit you, I say thank you for all your hard work.

Now it is time to get you stronger! The trip to the past was necessary for your unclogging and unchaining the issues that may have damaged, crippled, or stifled your ability to identify, communicate, or experience your emotions.

This chapter is going to take you to another level of experiencing your emotions and expanding your ability to feel any emotion you choose. Remember, emotions are not cognitions or thoughts. Emotions are an entirely different way through which we experience, process, and influence our environment and relationships.

Unlike work done learning in classical education, you cannot memorize an emotion and then have it the rest of your life. You have to experience an emotion. If you have laid the groundwork by identifying and communicating your emotions, what we are about to do will be much easier for you to grasp and experience.

Before we start this exercise, I want to take you back in time. I do not know about your life, but when I look back into mine, I see moments— some more providential than others—when I was going through an experience, but did not realize how powerful it was at the time, or how it would impact my future. For me, that "moment" was high school.

In high school, I did a lot of acting in school plays: *Othello, Macbeth, and Pillow Talk.* Along the way, we had a drama coach who walked us through some really strange exercises.

One of those exercises involved improvisation. He would give us a character and a situation, and we would have a minute with our partner to create a believable scene.

Another was an exercise that had to do with emotions. Our teacher had us lie down on the stage and then told us to get really quiet so we could feel the stillness through our entire body. This was the first time I ever remember focusing on one emotion. I distinctly remember feeling still and calm. I am certain this was the first time I knew my whole body could actually feel an emotion.

Then the teacher led us in guided meditation. Two of my takeaways from this exercise would later revolutionize my life and lead me further down the path to emotional fitness.

We are going to walk through these two takeaways, as they are truly integral to the body connection exercise we will be doing later in this chapter. Before I did the exercise of laying on that stage in my high school auditorium, I never thought I could choose to feel anything. I would have thought, like so many others, that feelings or emotions just happen.

Lying there on that black stage floor, I realized that I could choose to feel what someone was asking me to feel. I could choose to feel something. Never, in a thousand years, would I have guessed that I could, on demand, choose an emotion and actually command emotions. For me, this was extremely outside my experiential comfort zone.

My second major takeaway from this experience was that my whole body could feel this one feeling. Up to that point, if I became aware of a feeling, I would run it through my cognitive process to try to figure out what was going on with me emotionally.

I had no real access to identifying or feeling an emotion in my emotions. I could only sense emotions cognitively. This lack of emotional connectivity kept me stunted for years.

When I could actually give myself permission to feel a feeling, I was at least ten years older than I had been in my high school days. At that point, I was able to accelerate my emotional fitness significantly. Now I am able to feel an emotion, emotionally as well as physically, without fear or shame.

I say this because in the early stages of becoming emotionally fit, there were rules you were given or that you created to manage your limited emotional life. I will list a few of these below.

As you do the next two body connecting exercises, you may remember one of these rules, and if so, you may have to break it cognitively and experientially.

Rules

1. Feelings are for girls.

2. You cannot trust your feelings.

3. Feelings are for the weak.

4. Do not feel.

5. People will take advantage of you.

6. You will look ridiculous.

7. Feelings do not change anything.

8. Feelings are for cowards.

9. If you feel, you will lose control.

10. You cannot express your feelings well, so do not express them. You might embarrass yourself.

There are probably hundreds of other rules similar to these that you may come across as you do some of the emotional fitness exercises. As you think of these rules, make note of them. They will come to you as you are feeling or expanding your range of emotions.

These rules will come in the form of a voice in your head starting with, You shouldn't do this because... If such a message surfaces in your mind, you have found a rule. That is good news. It means you are going further than you ever have emotionally. If you listen to the rule, you will retreat and thus limit yourself from living an emotionally fit lifestyle. Simply put: Do not listen to the rule.

To break a rule, you can do a simple exercise I have given to clients for decades. This exercise is simple and effective.

Thank You and Goodbye Letter

Once you identify a rule that is limiting you emotionally, do two things. First, write both a thank you letter and goodbye letter to the rule. The rationale behind these two letters is the reality that your rule has been serving you in some way and helping you in your past or present world. You needed this rule to survive. However, things have changed. Now, you need to break this rule to live. The things that help us survive often limit us from living.

Let me give you an example of both types of letters. I will write my letters to the very straightforward rule that says, "Do not feel." This is a major rule if you come from a dysfunctional family or a family with a history of addiction.

Thank You

Dear Don't Feel,

I want to take a moment to thank you for serving me all these years. I know you came into my life very early because I needed you to protect me from mom and dad's insanity. You taught me very early to not feel because mom and dad couldn't handle my feelings, and so it would cost me more pain if I felt. You saved me from embarrassment with my family and friends and you probably saved me some spankings as well.

You were there in adolescence guarding me from rejection, fear, and a host of negative feelings. I just didn't have to feel them, and you have been working for me at work and in my marriage. I know I can just turn on the television or computer and leave this world like I used to as a child, all because of you.

Goodbye

Dear Don't Feel,

Although you helped me create this rule in my life, I have to say goodbye. Actually, I need to divorce you totally. You have kept me emotionally distant, aloof from friends, family, my spouse, and even my children. I hate you for not letting me be there, really there for the people I loved. You tricked me into believing that protecting me was more important than being there for them. You are a curse, not a blessing, and I command you to leave me forever. I may not know what it is like to live without you, but I am 100 percent committed to finding out. So goodbye, good riddance, and do not ever come back. I will no longer be your host!

Every family has different rules about emotions. In the spaces below, write out a few of the rules that existed in your family while you were growing up.

1._____

2._____

3._____

4._____

5._____

Which of the rules above are not helping you today?

1   2   3   4   5

To which of the rules in your family do you need to write a thank you and goodbye letter?

1   2   3   4   5

I find people, including myself, do much better accomplishing things if they commit to a date to get something done. On which day will you finish your thank you and goodbye letters?

_____/_____/_____

The Body

In this exercise, we are going to go back to the stage floor I mentioned earlier. We are going to visit our bodies and experience our emotions through our bodies. Honestly, the next few pages will include the preliminary work that some like to avoid on the way to emotional fitness.

Unfortunately, avoiding this work is like a football player avoiding the gym. I encourage you to not only read this section but do the exercises. Then you will get the results of emotional fitness. Those who have set time aside on a weekly or daily basis until they have done all or most of the emotions on their list have never regretted the time they spent investing in their emotional skill, confidence, and management of emotions.

In the previous chapter, we used six emotions for emotion identification. Since you have already identified these emotions and, hopefully, communicated them to someone, we will continue to use these emotions for all three body exercises. Your body holds emotions and helps you experience your emotions fully.

Feeling the Emotions

In this exercise, I want you to lie on the floor and relax. Give yourself a minute or so to feel relaxed, allowing the floor to fully support you. Then, take one emotion at a time and allow your body to feel that emotion. Feeling an emotion in your body is different than thinking a feeling. So relax, and give yourself a minute to feel the emotion.

The first emotion I want you to feel is calm. Just let yourself feel calm in your body. Once you feel calm in your body, you can hold it as long as you like.

The second emotion I want you to feel in your body is frustration. This should be significantly different than calm. When you feel frustration in your body, allow yourself permission to hold this emotion for as long as you wish.

The next emotion I want you to feel while you are lying on the floor is boldness. Let your body feel this emotion as long as you wish, but let your whole body feel bold.

This next emotion is a fun one to experience in your body. Feel the emotion of amusement in your whole body.

Creative is a totally different emotion than amused. Lay relaxed and let yourself experience creative in your body. When your body feels this creativity, allow yourself to hold it for as long as you wish.

The last feeling for you to feel in the floor exercise is eagerness. So experience eagerness in your whole body and then hold this emotion for as long as you desire.

Congratulations, if you have spent the last 10-20 minutes feeling your emotions, you have made a huge step in the right direction. Your body's emotional connection is critical to you being able to be emotionally fit.

I completed the feeling emotions exercise in my body on:
_____/_____/_____

Mime

In the 70s, there was a media fad I remember fondly: Marcel Marceau. He became the rage for quite a while, making appearances on numerous talk shows and in big media events.

What Marcel Marceau did was quite simple, but he was simply amazing at doing what he did. He would captivate audiences everywhere with his ability to mime.

When he did his skits, you both saw and felt what he was doing. A mime does not talk, but instead uses the body and face to communicate and express emotion. I remember one skit where an event made the mime sad. His sadness was so well expressed it felt completely real. Decades later, I still remember that expression.

Mime has much to do with emotional fitness. Miming will become a critical tool in your tool kit as you accelerate in your emotional fitness. Miming allows your body to feel the emotion passively, but as in the last exercise, it also allows you to fully engage and expand your body's ability to experience and express an emotion. Since this is something you need to experience in order to understand, I am going to ask you to do some miming.

Before we begin, honestly assess which one of the following two categories you are in:

The wishers category. These wish they could be emotionally fit. They wish they could feel or master their emotions but they are unwilling to do the work. A weight wisher is someone who wants to lose weight but does not change habits or do the work necessary to lose weight. Weight wishers will not lose weight. They want magic to change them instead of taking personal responsibility to make changes to get the real results.

The wanters category. These people make a plan, do the work, and keep doing the work until the results arrive. Unlike the wishers, they take personal responsibility, refuse to make excuses, and so always get the results they want. I believe that if you are this far in the book, you must want emotional fitness.

I want you to practice miming as we go through the next couple of pages. I warmed you up in the last exercise, so your body already has a familiarity with the experience of these emotions.

When you mime, it is best for you to be alone so you can in no way be inhibited or self-conscious. Put your body in a position to express an emotion. For example, if you were expressing excitement, you might stand up with your arms raised while you let excitement run through your entire body.

You can sit, stand, lie down, or put your body in any position to express an emotion. Remember, acting as a mime would, you will use your face to express the emotion. So much so that if someone were to look at you, they could probably guess the emotion you are experiencing.

It is important that when you actually feel the emotion in your body that you hold the feeling for fifteen seconds (make sure to use a timer). Then take a five-second break. After the break, go back to that same emotion until you feel it in your body again. Repeat the miming process until you feel it in your body for fifteen seconds. Then take your last break and stop miming the emotion.

For example, first we are miming the feeling of excitement. Excited (held for fifteen seconds), break, excited (held for fifteen seconds), break, excited (held for fifteen seconds). As you do each mime, try to allow your body to express the emotion <u>more</u> each time.

This exercise is powerful for you and your body. Over time, you can go through every emotion on the emotion list in the Appendix, and you will be extremely connected to your emotions—more connected than you ever imagined.

Find a place to be by yourself, locate a way to time yourself, and then practice miming the six emotions listed below. We will do the same six feelings you just completed in the feeling the emotion exercise.

1. Calm
2. Frustration
3. Boldness
4. Amusement
5. Creativity
6. Eagerness

I completed these mime exercises on _____/_____/_____

If you completed this exercise (and I hope you did), you just had your first intentional emotional fitness workout. You took responsibility and time and added a skill. Now you have a result.

You can feel! Your body can feel! You can learn to feel and you can learn as much as you want. To help you move more toward emotionally fitness, carve out fifteen minutes a day and do five mimes a day. In one month, your ability to feel emotions in your body will expand greatly. You will no longer fear emotions; you will be able to actually feel them. You can become more emotionally confident and expressive in just thirty days.

I can commit to fifteen minutes a day in the month of _____, and that time will be _____ am/pm.

Muscle Up

All of us have stubborn muscles that are difficult to grow or stretch; for me, it is my calves. My calves require three times as much work as any other muscle in my body. To muscle up my calves I had to go through a process.

First, I had to accept my calves were different and difficult. Second, I had to make a plan. Third, I had to do the extra work for a sustained period of time. Every time I muscled up, I was amazed my calves would grow or stretch depending on my focus.

Every person I have worked with has emotions that are weak or have a limited range. Sometimes this is because of family of origin rules, sometimes because of a traumatic experience, or sometimes simply because the particular emotion may never have been worked before.

As you go through the mime exercises with the emotion list in the Appendix, you will come across emotions that are challenging for you. When you do, highlight these emotions. Note them as emotions you will want to muscle up on. You might muscle up one time or muscle up for a week depending on your needs.

The muscle up exercise is easier to explain than do because we tend to run from hard emotions. I encourage you to muscle up so that any emotion that has been weak, unmanageable, or unexpressed can become an emotional strength for you.

Muscle up is simple. You put yourself in the mime and first hold it for fifteen seconds, break, then hold the emotion in your body for thirty seconds, break, then for forty-five seconds, break, and then one minute. You can continue this for up to two minutes if you have a very stubborn emotion. Each time you go back to the mime, try to go deeper into the emotion and expand the experience and expression of that emotion.

An example of a common difficult feeling is rejection. You would mime rejection as directed above (fifteen, thirty, forty-five, and sixty seconds). This exercise will allow you the experience of feeling these challenging emotions fully. You do not have to act on them. You are the master of them. Your emotional mastery is a key element in being and staying emotionally fit for the rest of your life.

Before you did the muscle up exercise, you circled your more challenging emotions while doing the mime exercise, working through the emotions list in the Appendix. As you do a muscle up on that feeling, place an X over the feeling because you have done the work for more emotionally mastery.

When I do the muscle up exercise, I really push myself to feel the emotion fully. I let my whole body feel the emotion, and then I push to feel it more and more intensely. I am absolutely blown away by how far I can intentionally expand my emotional range. I have had many deep experiences with the muscle up exercise, so I really encourage you to not shortchange yourself when doing it.

I want you to play the game of living life well emotionally. To play well, you must practice well, so practice well to live well. I am proud of every minute you put into your emotional fitness.

Switch

Most of us have felt as though we have been ridden by our emotions. You know the feeling when something such as anger, fear, or aloneness overwhelmingly grabs you by the hand and runs with you. It is much like a much bigger brother or sister taking you by the hand when you are small and running at their full speed with you in tow. You no longer have control of where or how fast you are going. We have all had an embarrassing moment when an emotion has taken us to a place in which we said or did something very unwise, unfriendly, or just generally out of character.

Especially strong emotions have the potential to grab your mind, will, and sadly, your speech, and take you for a ride. The ride is not always fun and can really hurt you or severely hurt those you love.

For some of you, the experience of your emotions taking your for a ride is rare or only happens under a particular set of circumstances. However, for others, being taken for a ride by their emotions happens regularly, even daily.

Regardless of whether this whisking away happens rarely or regularly, there is hope. You can actually live an emotionally fit lifestyle where you can choose your emotions. This may not seem feasible, but I assure you this skill is just moments away.

April is a lovely woman in her thirties. She just quit her job after having her second child. In her job, April was competent and appreciated by her employers and those who reported to her. She always seemed to have it all together. At home, April was a completely different story. She had some emotions over which she had zero management. It was like, instead of being grabbed by the hand by an older brother or sister, she was grabbed by a train. This feeling hit her so fast she would explode, yell, curse, and rant.

April found the emotions of frustration and overwhelming futility to be really unmanageable for her. What is worse, she really wanted to be a better mother than her mom had been. Her mother had a reputation for being difficult and frustrating. April wanted to be different and she succeeded. She found the switch, and with practice within a couple weeks, she was able to not only master the emotions of frustration and overwhelming futility, but found a couple other emotions that were affecting other areas in her life.

Justin was a mostly well-adjusted senior in college. He did well in his academic pursuits, was pretty social, and had a close group of buddies he hung around. Justin just broke up with a girlfriend of eight months after finding out she had cheated on him. At first, he thought he would be fine, but instead, he declined quickly. He found himself going to bars, getting drunk, missing classes and work, and becoming depressed. Justin found the feeling of rejection to be paralyzing.

When talking with Justin, it was clear this was not the first time he had been rejected. The girl he was dating was the first girl he had gotten into a relationship with in the last three years. Before then, he had dated a girl in high school who had dumped him. She was his first "true love." The pain went even deeper with Justin. His mom had an online relationship that led to an affair, and she left her family to move to another state when he was fourteen years old.

You can see in Justin's story how rejection would be so difficult for him to manage. He saw that his lack of mastering rejection would be a problem long-term if he could not solve it. Fortunately, Justin was able to find the switch and master rejection and reengage in the dating process.

I have shared stories of other people. Now I want to tell you a couple stories about myself. The first story I will share with you is how I found the switch. The second story is how I used the switch and have kept using it.

Like most people, I have several titles. But the two most important titles I have are husband and father. The husband title comes with some expectations, one being that I will be a handyman around the house. Though I am not necessarily the most handy of men, I get a lot of things done.

One of the things I do is stain the wood around the front of my house. Every few years I need to do this. I start by sanding down the old stain, then paint on the new stain, and finally seal it. The best part about this process is that the window in the front of my house is more than twenty feet high. This means I have to use a sixteen-foot ladder and stand on top of it to access the top of the window. This would work fine except for the fact I have a rosebush just where I need to place the ladder. One day, I did what any guy would do: I jammed the ladder into the rosebush with one leg of the ladder on the ground and the other slightly suspended by the branches on the rosebush.

As you can imagine, the ladder became increasingly unstable the higher I worked. As I traveled up and down it, the feeling that I was unsafe began to build. This bothered me. Being who I am, I was intrigued by this feeling because very rarely do I feel unsafe. I asked myself why I was feeling this way and discovered that my emotional response made sense since my ladder was unstable and I had a twenty-foot drop to the concrete below.

I knew I had to finish the project, so I had to solve my internal problem. I tried an experiment I call "the switch" and it worked—really well. Instead of feeling unsafe, I choose to feel confident. I was able to keep choosing confident and I was able to finish the job and feel confident instead of unsafe.

Here is another story of mine with which you might identify. I was sitting in the airport waiting for my connecting flight. The flight was already boarding, so I asked a man standing in line which group was boarding. He told me group one was boarding. My boarding pass was stamped "group one," so I proceeded to the gate attendant and she took one look at my pass and politely, but firmly told me they were only boarding first class and that I needed to stand aside.

Immediately, I could feel embarrassment rush though my body. Since I know and practice the switch, I just chose to feel calm. All the feelings of embarrassment and self-concern left my body and I was able to go through the rest of the boarding procedure with a smile and not one more negative thought.

The Switch

As we discussed before, one of my most important titles is father. As a father, I get assigned some very stereotypical functions, especially around Christmas. On Christmas Day, after all the gifts have been opened, it is typically my job to untie the gifts from their boxes and put them together.

One Christmas, my son Jubal received many Thomas the Train gifts. So Jubal and I created several options to design his new train track until we settled on one using a piece called a switcher. This piece looked totally different than all the other tracks we had put together. On it was a little red lever so you could decide which way the train was going to proceed on the track. If you pushed the lever in towards the track, the train would make a left. If you pulled the lever out, the train went to the right. The switch determined the direction of the train.

Think about a simple light switch for a moment. You flip it on and the lights turn on. You switch it off, energy is stopped, and the light stays dark. Similarly, you and I can have an emotional switch. This switch can serve us in both capacities. Like the train, it can help us intentionally decide which emotion we want to have and go in that direction. Then once practiced, the switch can allow us to turn off the energy to the unwanted emotion and instead decide to give it to an emotion of our choice.

The switch is powerful. Since I found my switch and have been able to practice it, I can use it at will in a variety of situations. I can choose creativity when previously I felt stuck. I can choose relaxed instead of frustrated, and compassion instead of anger.

Since this discovery, I have changed my emotions from unappreciated to loved in relationships. Imagine how I act, think, and speak when I choose loved instead of unappreciated by someone. Imagine living like this at work, home, or out and about. I have fun with my switch, and, as the master of my emotions, I can choose my emotions anytime, even if I am tired.

To find and practice your switch, you are going to have to do three switching exercises. Just reading this section will not help your emotional fitness in any way. If you decide to do the following exercise, you can find your switch and embark on an endless experiment of switching your emotions at will.

Switching is a helpful technique to use when addressing difficult emotions. Remember April's frustration of overwhelming futility and how she was able to switch to calm, competent, and hopeful after finding her switch? Similarly, Justin was able to move from rejection to desired, amazing, and loved after he found his switch.

To do this switch and have it be meaningful, you would pick from some of the feelings you mimed and then muscled up on. If you have not done those exercises, I would strongly recommend you do them before starting this exercise.

For those of you who have experienced some difficult feelings through mime, list those feelings and the opposite feeling.

Your Feeling
(i.e. frustrated)

Opposite Feeling
(i.e. calm)

1._____   1._____

2._____   2._____

3._____   3._____

4._____   4._____

For those of you who have to discover your challenging feelings, I would like you to use the following feelings for this exercise.

1. Frustration	1. Calm
2. Intimidated	2. Confident
3. Rejected	3. Accepted
4. Alone	4. Close

In the space below, write down your first feeling and its opposite. If you are unable to access a feeling, choose frustration and calm as your opposite pair.

1._____   1._____

Now mime your first feeling (or frustrated) just like you have done before. Get your body in a position where it feels frustrated, hold this fifteen seconds, and then take a small 5-10 second break. Then hold two more times with breaks between them. This will be easy for you if you have been practicing. Now, mime the second, opposite feeling (calm). Do the same mime three times with a 5-10 second break between each one. Then take a break.

After your break, I want you to mime the first feeling for fifteen seconds, take no break, then switch to the opposite feeling with no breaks in between. Then switch back to the first feeling, take no break, go to the opposite feeling, take no break, go back to the first feeling, then switch to the second feeling.

Let me show you what this should look like:

Step One: Frustrated, break, frustrated, break, frustrated

Step Two: Calm, break, calm, break, calm

Step Three: Frustrated, calm, frustrated, calm, frustrated, calm, break (no breaks in-between miming)

Take a moment and write down what you experienced in this switch exercise.

I experienced: _____

_____

_____

Now I want you to repeat the process with your second feeling and its opposite, following step one, step two, and step three.

Feeling 2   **Opposite Feeling**

Follow that with your third and fourth feeling and their opposite feelings.

Feeling 3   **Opposite Feeling**

Feeling 4   **Opposite Feeling**

On what date did you complete all four feelings and switch to the opposite feeling? _____/_____/_____

Take a moment and write down what you experienced. _____

_____

_____

_____

_____

What do you think about being able to better access and allow your body to feel emotions on demand? How do you feel about this?

I think: _____

_____

I feel: _____

_____

What do you think about actually experiencing polar opposite emotions while still being able to manage your emotions? How do you feel about this?

I think: _____

_____

I feel: _____

_____

What do you think about the fact you could actually switch how you feel on demand? How do you feel about this?

I think: _____

_____

I feel: _____

_____

After doing a few switches, many of my clients can actually feel or experience their switch. This ability to decide to feel differently at will is life-changing. I hope you had the opportunity to switch as well.

I used this exercise as I was writing this chapter. My son and I were traveling together, and I arrived on the plane before he did. I had his carry-on bag along with mine. I was fortunate enough to get a front row seat, but unfortunately, it did not have an overhead bin. The flight attendant greeted me at the door and abruptly informed me I had to gate check one of my bags because my two would take up too much space.

I felt offended because I had chosen bags specifically for smaller planes that I knew would fit in the overhead bin. I knew I had a right to my bags on the plane, and I had just paid extra to get on this earlier flight. As I sat there, I realized I did not like or want to be offended.

The flight attendant did not know I paid extra to be on the flight. She did not know my son was joining me and that I had his bag. She was just being thoughtful toward the group of people boarding, and I had no idea what her day had been or her story was. I decided to feel kind and compassionate toward her as a person. When I switched my emotions, I changed the whole rest of my flight and had a better day by not carrying around the offended emotion.

Once you practice enough mimes, find your challenging feelings, muscle up, and then find and use your switch, you can be emotionally fit enough to change your days, your relationships, and how you want to feel and behave at any given moment.

The switch allows you to choose emotions, not be a victim of your emotions or a passenger in its car. Instead, with the switch, you have the steering wheel in your hand. The switch does not take away emotions like those I shared in the earlier plane story. I truly did feel embarrassed, but I switched. Like the story above, I truly felt offended, but I chose compassion. When I chose compassion, I loosened up and was able to focus on writing this book.

Having a switch is a powerful and necessary tool for becoming and staying emotionally fit. Having a switch is like finding you have a hidden talent. It is like discovering you can draw, sing, sculpt, or cook. The switch gives you that moment of feeling like you can do it.

When I was in fifth grade, my mom bought me some books on how to draw animals. One book had the steps for drawing animals broken down by drawing familiar shapes. Using it, I began drawing. The next thing I knew, I could draw a horse, squirrel, and other animals. I remember being amazed and proud that I could draw. Until then, I had never realized I had the ability to draw. I practiced my new skill for a few weeks.

Like my fifth grade experience, those of you who did the switch exercise had an amazing, proud experience. You found your switch! For most of you, you must practice using your switch. If not, you will be left with just the experience, and years from now you will be less likely to know where your switch is and less likely to use it when it would be in your best interest.

To get and stay emotionally fit, you have to decide to practice at least the next 60-90 days, working your way through the emotions list, miming and muscling up. Then after muscling up on an emotion, you must do a switch. Over these next few months, you will feel amazingly more emotionally literate and competent.

Having an emotionally fit lifestyle will feel and become amazing to you. This is an exciting stage of growth and change. I call it your climb stage. In this stage, you are focused, diligent, and seeing positive changes.

Your next stage of growth and change is totally up to you. It could decline. You could stop doing any practice or using your emotional fitness skills. You could find yourself experiencing and sharing your emotions less. You could go back to more of a functional way of living, with only intermittent connectedness in your life. It could look like a plateau where you are definitely better off than you used to be. Like weight loss, this position is much like maintaining the twenty pound weight loss, but not getting more fit.

You might be a continual grower. You do not have to make the same commitment you did in the growth stages, but you practice emotions identification and communication fairly regularly. You might mime or muscle up occasionally, and you are able to use your switch and sometimes even play with it to change your day or relationships. You are emotionally fit. You can feel it daily and yet you stretch yourself here and there to keep your emotional muscles alive and toned.

I am proud of how far you have come on your journey to becoming emotionally fit. If you have been practicing, you deserve a high five. You have done the work to be on your journey of emotional fitness, and every day you are transforming yourself from an emotional glob to a well-defined, emotionally healthy being.

The Journey

It has been amazing to walk with you through learning what an emotion is and is not, how to identify an emotion, how to communicate, mime, and power up emotionally. As you practice, you will become increasingly emotionally fit.

What follows is a sixty day journal you can use to record your progress. Believe me, it will help you stay focused. As you work on your journal, you will see daily incremental growth. Before I give you the journal, I want to give you examples to help you. The two examples will be from Charles' and Angela's perspective.

The 60-Day Emotional Fitness Journal will help you keep track of how you are applying your emotional fitness skills in various environments: home, work, school, primary social circle, and out and about.

Charles is a middle-aged corporate executive. He is married and has two teenage daughters.

Charles' Log

At work, Charles felt tense before a meeting with an underperforming employee. He felt surprised when his favorite coffee shop unexpectedly began to offer a seasonal pumpkin spice drink. He felt exhilarated when Tom, a coworker, told him the profit on a project he was working on put him in for a bonus next month. He also communicated feeling proud of his key team members after receiving Tom's information.

| **Identified:** | 1.Tense | 2.Surprised |
| **Communicated:** | 1. Exhilarated | 2. Proud |

At home, he identified that he felt endeared to his oldest daughter who sent a video to his phone of her doing something silly. He also identified the feeling of frustration in response to his garage door opener battery going dead, causing him to park in front of the house and walk up the sidewalk in the rain. Charles communicated feeling thankful to his wife who was able to pick up his younger daughter, allowing him to run a quick errand. He also communicated feeling challenged when helping his daughter figure out her math assignment.

Identified: 1. Endeared   2. Frustrated
Communicated: 1. Thankful   2. Challenged

Out and about, Charles identified feeling chatty with a favorite waiter at a restaurant where he regularly has his lunch. He also felt content sipping his pumpkin spice latté in the morning. He communicated that he felt pushed today by his racquetball partner, and feeling awkward as he had to make a correction on his deposit slip at the bank.

Identified: 1. Chatty   2. Content
Communicated: 1. Pushed   2. Awkward

Angela is a twenty-year-old college student. She grew up in an alcoholic home and lives in the dorm at her college. Angela is dating Troy and works at a pizza parlor as a waitress.

Angela's Log

In her dorm room, Angela realized she was feeling a little alone. Not alone like when her roommate was not there, but alone like she missed her brother, sister, and dog. She also identified that she felt cramped, moving around her roommate's clutter to find something she needed. She commented to her roommate how excited she felt about how things were going with Troy. She also communicated disgust with a girl on their floor who had left a mess in their common shower.

Identified: 1. Alone   2. Cramped
Communicated: 1. Excited   2. Disgust

At work, Angela identified feeling badgered by a coworker who goes to another school. She also felt cared for because some of her regulars asked her how school was going and were truly interested in her answer. She communicated feeling overwhelmed to another waitress after a team of high schoolers came to the pizza parlor. She communicated feeling rushed to get everything done by 10 p.m. because Troy was meeting her after work.

| Identified: | 1. Badgered | 2. Cared for |
| Communicated: | 1. Overwhelmed | 2. Rushed |

Out and about, on her way to class, Angela realized she had forgotten her car keys again and would need them right after class. She identified feeling forgetful. She also identified feeling buried in history class. She communicated feeling stuck on one of her papers to another student. After a big test, she communicated feeling free while getting her weekly smoothie.

| Identified: | 1. Forgetful | 2. Buried |
| Communicated: | 1. Stuck | 2. Free |

We all have emotions all day long. The 60-Day Emotional Fitness Journal helps you track what you are feeling. In this journal, you have a place to make notes on the other emotions you wrote out for emotions identification, your two emotions you intentionally share with someone and the number of emotions you mimed, muscled up, and/or practiced switching.

I know this will take some time, but the results can really be life-changing for you and those around you. I will leave you to work on your sixty day journal; then I will leave you with a closing word.

Emotional Fitness Journal　　　　🕙 Day 1

Home:

Identified　　　　＿＿＿＿＿＿＿＿＿＿　　　　＿＿＿＿＿＿＿＿＿＿

Communicated ＿＿＿＿＿＿＿＿＿＿　　　　＿＿＿＿＿＿＿＿＿＿

Work, school, primary social circle:

Identified　　　　＿＿＿＿＿＿＿＿＿＿　　　　＿＿＿＿＿＿＿＿＿＿

Communicated ＿＿＿＿＿＿＿＿＿＿　　　　＿＿＿＿＿＿＿＿＿＿

Out and About:

Identified　　　　＿＿＿＿＿＿＿＿＿＿　　　　＿＿＿＿＿＿＿＿＿＿

Communicated ＿＿＿＿＿＿＿＿＿＿　　　　＿＿＿＿＿＿＿＿＿＿

Feelings I wrote out today:

_____   _____

_____   _____

Feelings I practiced communicating (both present and past tense):

_____   _____

Feelings I mimed:

_____   _____

_____   _____

Feelings I muscled up:

_____   _____

_____   _____

Feelings I switched:

_____   _____

_____   _____

What did I learn about myself today?

_____

_____

Day 2

Home:

Identified   _____   _____

Communicated _____   _____

Work, school, primary social circle:

Identified   _____   _____

Communicated _____   _____

Out and About:

Identified   _____   _____

Communicated _____   _____

Feelings I wrote out today:

_____   _____

_____   _____

Feelings I practiced communicating (both present and past tense):

_____   _____

Feelings I mimed:

_____   _____

_____   _____

Feelings I muscled up:

_____   _____

_____   _____

Feelings I switched:

_____   _____

_____   _____

What did I learn about myself today?

_____

_____

Day 3

Home:

Identified   _____   _____

Communicated _____   _____

Work, school, primary social circle:

Identified   _____   _____

Communicated _____   _____

Out and About:

Identified   _____   _____

Communicated _____   _____

Feelings I wrote out today:

_____   _____

_____   _____

Feelings I practiced communicating (both present and past tense):

_____   _____

Feelings I mimed:

_____   _____

_____   _____

Feelings I muscled up:

_____   _____

_____   _____

Feelings I switched:

_____   _____

_____   _____

What did I learn about myself today?

_____

_____

⏱ Day 4

Home:

Identified   _____   _____

Communicated _____   _____

Work, school, primary social circle:

Identified   _____   _____

Communicated _____   _____

Out and About:

Identified   _____   _____

Communicated _____   _____

Feelings I wrote out today:

_____   _____

_____   _____

Feelings I practiced communicating (both present and past tense):

_____   _____

Feelings I mimed:

_____   _____

_____   _____

Feelings I muscled up:

_____   _____

_____   _____

Feelings I switched:

_____   _____

_____   _____

What did I learn about myself today?

_____

_____

🕰 Day 5

Home:

Identified   _____   _____

Communicated _____   _____

Work, school, primary social circle:

Identified   _____   _____

Communicated _____   _____

Out and About:

Identified   _____   _____

Communicated _____   _____

Feelings I wrote out today:

_____   _____

_____   _____

Feelings I practiced communicating (both present and past tense):

_____   _____

Feelings I mimed:

_____   _____

_____   _____

Feelings I muscled up:

_____   _____

_____   _____

Feelings I switched:

_____   _____

_____   _____

What did I learn about myself today?

_____

_____

Day 6

Home:

Identified _____ _____

Communicated _____ _____

Work, school, primary social circle:

Identified _____ _____

Communicated _____ _____

Out and About:

Identified _____ _____

Communicated _____ _____

Feelings I wrote out today:

_____ _____

_____ _____

Feelings I practiced communicating (both present and past tense):

_____ _____

Feelings I mimed:

_____ _____

_____ _____

Feelings I muscled up:

_____   _____

_____   _____

Feelings I switched:

_____   _____

_____   _____

What did I learn about myself today?

_____

_____

Day 7

Home:

Identified   _____   _____

Communicated _____   _____

Work, school, primary social circle:

Identified   _____   _____

Communicated _____   _____

Out and About:

Identified   _____   _____

Communicated _____   _____

Feelings I wrote out today:

_____   _____

_____   _____

Feelings I practiced communicating (both present and past tense):

_____   _____

Feelings I mimed:

_____   _____

_____   _____

Feelings I muscled up:

_____   _____

_____   _____

Feelings I switched:

_____   _____

_____   _____

What did I learn about myself today?

_____

_____

⚙ Day 8

Home:

Identified   _____   _____

Communicated _____   _____

Work, school, primary social circle:

Identified   _____   _____

Communicated _____   _____

Out and About:

Identified   _____   _____

Communicated _____   _____

Feelings I wrote out today:

_____   _____

_____   _____

Feelings I practiced communicating (both present and past tense):

_____   _____

Feelings I mimed:

_____   _____

_____   _____

Feelings I muscled up:

_____   _____

_____   _____

Feelings I switched:

_____   _____

_____   _____

What did I learn about myself today?

_____

_____

Day 9

                    Home:

Identified   _____   _____

Communicated _____   _____

                    Work, school, primary social circle:

Identified   _____   _____

Communicated _____   _____

                    Out and About:

Identified   _____   _____

Communicated _____   _____

Feelings I wrote out today:

_____   _____

_____   _____

Feelings I practiced communicating (both present and past tense):

_____   _____

Feelings I mimed:

_____   _____

_____   _____

Feelings I muscled up:

_____   _____

_____   _____

Feelings I switched:

_____   _____

_____   _____

What did I learn about myself today?

_____

_____

Day 10

Home:

Identified _____   _____

Communicated _____   _____

Work, school, primary social circle:

Identified _____   _____

Communicated _____   _____

Out and About:

Identified _____   _____

Communicated _____   _____

Feelings I wrote out today:

_____   _____

_____   _____

Feelings I practiced communicating (both present and past tense):

_____   _____

Feelings I mimed:

_____   _____

_____   _____

Feelings I muscled up:

_____ _____

_____ _____

Feelings I switched:

_____ _____

_____ _____

What did I learn about myself today?

_____

_____

Day 11

Home:

Identified _____ _____

Communicated _____ _____

Work, school, primary social circle:

Identified _____ _____

Communicated _____ _____

Out and About:

Identified _____ _____

Communicated _____ _____

Feelings I wrote out today:

_____   _____

_____   _____

Feelings I practiced communicating (both present and past tense):

_____   _____

Feelings I mimed:

_____   _____

_____   _____

Feelings I muscled up:

_____   _____

_____   _____

Feelings I switched:

_____   _____

_____   _____

What did I learn about myself today?

_____

_____

Day 12

Home:

Identified _____ _____

Communicated _____ _____

Work, school, primary social circle:

Identified _____ _____

Communicated _____ _____

Out and About:

Identified _____ _____

Communicated _____ _____

Feelings I wrote out today:

_____ _____

_____ _____

Feelings I practiced communicating (both present and past tense):

_____ _____

Feelings I mimed:

_____ _____

_____ _____

Feelings I muscled up:

_____   _____

_____   _____

Feelings I switched:

_____   _____

_____   _____

What did I learn about myself today?

_____

_____

Day 13

Home:

Identified   _____   _____

Communicated _____   _____

Work, school, primary social circle:

Identified   _____   _____

Communicated _____   _____

Out and About:

Identified   _____   _____

Communicated _____   _____

Feelings I wrote out today:

_____   _____

_____   _____

Feelings I practiced communicating (both present and past tense):

_____   _____

Feelings I mimed:

_____   _____

_____   _____

Feelings I muscled up:

_____   _____

_____   _____

Feelings I switched:

_____   _____

_____   _____

What did I learn about myself today?

_____

_____

Day 14

Home:

Identified   _____   _____

Communicated _____   _____

Work, school, primary social circle:

Identified   _____   _____

Communicated _____   _____

Out and About:

Identified   _____   _____

Communicated _____   _____

Feelings I wrote out today:

_____   _____

_____   _____

Feelings I practiced communicating (both present and past tense):

_____   _____

Feelings I mimed:

_____   _____

_____   _____

Feelings I muscled up:

_____   _____

_____   _____

Feelings I switched:

_____   _____

_____   _____

What did I learn about myself today?

_____

_____

Day 15

Home:

Identified   _____   _____

Communicated _____   _____

Work, school, primary social circle:

Identified   _____   _____

Communicated _____   _____

Out and About:

Identified   _____   _____

Communicated _____   _____

Feelings I wrote out today:

_____   _____

_____   _____

Feelings I practiced communicating (both present and past tense):

_____   _____

Feelings I mimed:

_____   _____

_____   _____

Feelings I muscled up:

_____   _____

_____   _____

Feelings I switched:

_____   _____

_____   _____

What did I learn about myself today?

_____

_____

Home:

Identified   _____   _____

Communicated _____   _____

Work, school, primary social circle:

Identified   _____   _____

Communicated _____   _____

Out and About:

Identified   _____   _____

Communicated _____   _____

Feelings I wrote out today:

_____   _____

_____   _____

Feelings I practiced communicating (both present and past tense):

_____   _____

Feelings I mimed:

_____   _____

_____   _____

Feelings I muscled up:

_____   _____

_____   _____

Feelings I switched:

_____   _____

_____   _____

What did I learn about myself today?

_____

_____

🦎 Day 17

Home:

Identified   _____   _____

Communicated _____   _____

Work, school, primary social circle:

Identified   _____   _____

Communicated _____   _____

Out and About:

Identified   _____   _____

Communicated _____   _____

Feelings I wrote out today:

_____   _____

_____   _____

Feelings I practiced communicating (both present and past tense):

_____   _____

Feelings I mimed:

_____   _____

_____   _____

Feelings I muscled up:

_____   _____

_____   _____

Feelings I switched:

_____   _____

_____   _____

What did I learn about myself today?

_____

_____

Day 18

Home:

Identified   _____   _____

Communicated _____   _____

Work, school, primary social circle:

Identified   _____   _____

Communicated _____   _____

Out and About:

Identified   _____   _____

Communicated _____   _____

Feelings I wrote out today:

_____   _____

_____   _____

Feelings I practiced communicating (both present and past tense):

_____   _____

Feelings I mimed:

_____   _____

_____   _____

Feelings I muscled up:

_____   _____

_____   _____

Feelings I switched:

_____   _____

_____   _____

What did I learn about myself today?

_____

_____

Day 19

Home:

Identified   _____   _____

Communicated _____   _____

Work, school, primary social circle:

Identified   _____   _____

Communicated _____   _____

Out and About:

Identified   _____   _____

Communicated _____   _____

Feelings I wrote out today:

_____   _____

_____   _____

Feelings I practiced communicating (both present and past tense):

_____   _____

Feelings I mimed:

_____   _____

_____   _____

Feelings I muscled up:

_____   _____

_____   _____

Feelings I switched:

_____   _____

_____   _____

What did I learn about myself today?

_____

_____

Day 20

Home:

Identified   _____   _____

Communicated _____   _____

Work, school, primary social circle:

Identified   _____   _____

Communicated _____   _____

Out and About:

Identified   _____   _____

Communicated _____   _____

Feelings I wrote out today:

_____   _____

_____   _____

Feelings I practiced communicating (both present and past tense):

_____   _____

Feelings I mimed:

_____   _____

_____   _____

Feelings I muscled up:

_____   _____

_____   _____

Feelings I switched:

_____   _____

_____   _____

What did I learn about myself today?

_____

_____

Day 21

Home:

Identified   _____   _____

Communicated _____   _____

Work, school, primary social circle:

Identified   _____   _____

Communicated _____   _____

Out and About:

Identified   _____   _____

Communicated _____   _____

Feelings I wrote out today:

_____   _____

_____   _____

Feelings I practiced communicating (both present and past tense):

_____   _____

Feelings I mimed:

_____   _____

_____   _____

Feelings I muscled up:

_____   _____

_____   _____

Feelings I switched:

_____   _____

_____   _____

What did I learn about myself today?

_____

_____

Day 22

Home:

Identified _____   _____

Communicated _____   _____

Work, school, primary social circle:

Identified _____   _____

Communicated _____   _____

Out and About:

Identified _____   _____

Communicated _____   _____

Feelings I wrote out today:

_____   _____

_____   _____

Feelings I practiced communicating (both present and past tense):

_____   _____

Feelings I mimed:

_____   _____

_____   _____

Feelings I muscled up:

_____   _____

_____   _____

Feelings I switched:

_____   _____

_____   _____

What did I learn about myself today?

_____

_____

Day 23

Home:

Identified   _____   _____

Communicated _____   _____

Work, school, primary social circle:

Identified   _____   _____

Communicated _____   _____

Out and About:

Identified   _____   _____

Communicated _____   _____

Feelings I wrote out today:

_____   _____

_____   _____

Feelings I practiced communicating (both present and past tense):

_____   _____

Feelings I mimed:

_____   _____

_____   _____

Feelings I muscled up:

_____   _____

_____   _____

Feelings I switched:

_____   _____

_____   _____

What did I learn about myself today?

_____

_____

Day 24

Home:

Identified   _____   _____

Communicated _____   _____

Work, school, primary social circle:

Identified   _____   _____

Communicated _____   _____

Out and About:

Identified   _____   _____

Communicated _____   _____

Feelings I wrote out today:

_____   _____

_____   _____

Feelings I practiced communicating (both present and past tense):

_____   _____

Feelings I mimed:

_____   _____

_____   _____

Feelings I muscled up:

_____   _____

_____   _____

Feelings I switched:

_____   _____

_____   _____

What did I learn about myself today?

_____

_____

Day 25

Home:

Identified   _____   _____

Communicated _____   _____

Work, school, primary social circle:

Identified   _____   _____

Communicated _____   _____

Out and About:

Identified   _____   _____

Communicated _____   _____

Feelings I wrote out today:

_____   _____

_____   _____

Feelings I practiced communicating (both present and past tense):

_____   _____

Feelings I mimed:

_____   _____

_____   _____

Feelings I muscled up:

_____   _____

_____   _____

Feelings I switched:

_____   _____

_____   _____

What did I learn about myself today?

_____

_____

Day 26

Home:

Identified _____   _____

Communicated _____   _____

Work, school, primary social circle:

Identified _____   _____

Communicated _____   _____

Out and About:

Identified _____   _____

Communicated _____   _____

Feelings I wrote out today:

_____   _____

_____   _____

Feelings I practiced communicating (both present and past tense):

_____   _____

Feelings I mimed:

_____   _____

_____   _____

Feelings I muscled up:

_____   _____

_____   _____

Feelings I switched:

_____   _____

_____   _____

What did I learn about myself today?

_____

_____

Day 27

Home:

Identified   _____   _____

Communicated _____   _____

Work, school, primary social circle:

Identified   _____   _____

Communicated _____   _____

Out and About:

Identified   _____   _____

Communicated _____   _____

Feelings I wrote out today:

_____   _____

_____   _____

Feelings I practiced communicating (both present and past tense):

_____   _____

Feelings I mimed:

_____   _____

_____   _____

Feelings I muscled up:

_____   _____

_____   _____

Feelings I switched:

_____   _____

_____   _____

What did I learn about myself today?

_____

_____

Day 28

Home:

Identified _____ _____

Communicated _____ _____

Work, school, primary social circle:

Identified _____ _____

Communicated _____ _____

Out and About:

Identified _____ _____

Communicated _____ _____

Feelings I wrote out today:

_____ _____

_____ _____

Feelings I practiced communicating (both present and past tense):

_____ _____

Feelings I mimed:

_____ _____

_____ _____

Feelings I muscled up:

_____   _____

_____   _____

Feelings I switched:

_____   _____

_____   _____

What did I learn about myself today?

_____

_____

Day 29

Home:

Identified   _____   _____

Communicated _____   _____

Work, school, primary social circle:

Identified   _____   _____

Communicated _____   _____

Out and About:

Identified   _____   _____

Communicated _____   _____

Feelings I wrote out today:

_____   _____

_____   _____

Feelings I practiced communicating (both present and past tense):

_____   _____

Feelings I mimed:

_____   _____

_____   _____

Feelings I muscled up:

_____   _____

_____   _____

Feelings I switched:

_____   _____

_____   _____

What did I learn about myself today?

_____

_____

Day 30

Home:

Identified _____   _____

Communicated _____   _____

Work, school, primary social circle:

Identified _____   _____

Communicated _____   _____

Out and About:

Identified _____   _____

Communicated _____   _____

Feelings I wrote out today:

_____   _____

_____   _____

Feelings I practiced communicating (both present and past tense):

_____   _____

Feelings I mimed:

_____   _____

_____   _____

Feelings I muscled up:

_____   _____

_____   _____

Feelings I switched:

_____   _____

_____   _____

What did I learn about myself today?

_____

_____

🕛 Day 31

Home:

Identified   _____   _____

Communicated _____   _____

Work, school, primary social circle:

Identified   _____   _____

Communicated _____   _____

Out and About:

Identified   _____   _____

Communicated _____   _____

Feelings I wrote out today:

_____   _____

_____   _____

Feelings I practiced communicating (both present and past tense):

_____   _____

Feelings I mimed:

_____   _____

_____   _____

Feelings I muscled up:

_____   _____

_____   _____

Feelings I switched:

_____   _____

_____   _____

What did I learn about myself today?

_____

_____

Day 32

Home:

Identified _____ _____

Communicated _____ _____

Work, school, primary social circle:

Identified _____ _____

Communicated _____ _____

Out and About:

Identified _____ _____

Communicated _____ _____

Feelings I wrote out today:

_____ _____

_____ _____

Feelings I practiced communicating (both present and past tense):

_____ _____

Feelings I mimed:

_____ _____

_____ _____

Feelings I muscled up:

_____   _____

_____   _____

Feelings I switched:

_____   _____

_____   _____

What did I learn about myself today?

_____

_____

🕑 Day 33

Home:

Identified   _____   _____

Communicated _____   _____

Work, school, primary social circle:

Identified   _____   _____

Communicated _____   _____

Out and About:

Identified   _____   _____

Communicated _____   _____

Feelings I wrote out today:

_____   _____

_____   _____

Feelings I practiced communicating (both present and past tense):

_____   _____

Feelings I mimed:

_____   _____

_____   _____

Feelings I muscled up:

_____   _____

_____   _____

Feelings I switched:

_____   _____

_____   _____

What did I learn about myself today?

_____

_____

Day 34

Home:

Identified   _____   _____

Communicated _____   _____

Work, school, primary social circle:

Identified   _____   _____

Communicated _____   _____

Out and About:

Identified   _____   _____

Communicated _____   _____

Feelings I wrote out today:

_____   _____

_____   _____

Feelings I practiced communicating (both present and past tense):

_____   _____

Feelings I mimed:

_____   _____

_____   _____

Feelings I muscled up:

_____   _____

_____   _____

Feelings I switched:

_____   _____

_____   _____

What did I learn about myself today?

_____

_____

Day 35

Home:

Identified   _____   _____

Communicated _____   _____

Work, school, primary social circle:

Identified   _____   _____

Communicated _____   _____

Out and About:

Identified   _____   _____

Communicated _____   _____

Feelings I wrote out today:

_____   _____

_____   _____

Feelings I practiced communicating (both present and past tense):

_____   _____

Feelings I mimed:

_____   _____

_____   _____

Feelings I muscled up:

_____   _____

_____   _____

Feelings I switched:

_____   _____

_____   _____

What did I learn about myself today?

_____

_____

Day 36

Home:

Identified   _____   _____

Communicated _____   _____

Work, school, primary social circle:

Identified   _____   _____

Communicated _____   _____

Out and About:

Identified   _____   _____

Communicated _____   _____

Feelings I wrote out today:

_____   _____

_____   _____

Feelings I practiced communicating (both present and past tense):

_____   _____

Feelings I mimed:

_____   _____

_____   _____

Feelings I muscled up:

_____   _____

_____   _____

Feelings I switched:

_____   _____

_____   _____

What did I learn about myself today?

_____

_____

Day 37

Home:

Identified   _____   _____

Communicated _____   _____

Work, school, primary social circle:

Identified   _____   _____

Communicated _____   _____

Out and About:

Identified   _____   _____

Communicated _____   _____

Feelings I wrote out today:

_____   _____

_____   _____

Feelings I practiced communicating (both present and past tense):

_____   _____

Feelings I mimed:

_____   _____

_____   _____

Feelings I muscled up:

_____   _____

_____   _____

Feelings I switched:

_____   _____

_____   _____

What did I learn about myself today?

_____

_____

Day 38

Home:

Identified   _____   _____

Communicated _____   _____

Work, school, primary social circle:

Identified   _____   _____

Communicated _____   _____

Out and About:

Identified   _____   _____

Communicated _____   _____

Feelings I wrote out today:

_____   _____

_____   _____

Feelings I practiced communicating (both present and past tense):

_____   _____

Feelings I mimed:

_____   _____

_____   _____

Feelings I muscled up:

_____   _____

_____   _____

Feelings I switched:

_____   _____

_____   _____

What did I learn about myself today?

_____

_____

Day 39

Home:

Identified   _____   _____

Communicated _____   _____

Work, school, primary social circle:

Identified   _____   _____

Communicated _____   _____

Out and About:

Identified   _____   _____

Communicated _____   _____

Feelings I wrote out today:

_____   _____

_____   _____

Feelings I practiced communicating (both present and past tense):

_____   _____

Feelings I mimed:

_____   _____

_____   _____

Feelings I muscled up:

_____   _____

_____   _____

Feelings I switched:

_____   _____

_____   _____

What did I learn about myself today?

_____

_____

Day 40

Home:

Identified   _____   _____

Communicated _____   _____

Work, school, primary social circle:

Identified   _____   _____

Communicated _____   _____

Out and About:

Identified   _____   _____

Communicated _____   _____

Feelings I wrote out today:

_____   _____

_____   _____

Feelings I practiced communicating (both present and past tense):

_____   _____

Feelings I mimed:

_____   _____

_____   _____

Feelings I muscled up:

_____   _____

_____   _____

Feelings I switched:

_____   _____

_____   _____

What did I learn about myself today?

_____

_____

Day 41

Home:

Identified   _____   _____

Communicated _____   _____

Work, school, primary social circle:

Identified   _____   _____

Communicated _____   _____

Out and About:

Identified   _____   _____

Communicated _____   _____

Feelings I wrote out today:

_____   _____

_____   _____

Feelings I practiced communicating (both present and past tense):

_____   _____

Feelings I mimed:

_____   _____

_____   _____

Feelings I muscled up:

_____   _____

_____   _____

Feelings I switched:

_____   _____

_____   _____

What did I learn about myself today?

_____

_____

Day 42

Home:

Identified   _____   _____

Communicated _____   _____

Work, school, primary social circle:

Identified   _____   _____

Communicated _____   _____

Out and About:

Identified   _____   _____

Communicated _____   _____

Feelings I wrote out today:

_____   _____

_____   _____

Feelings I practiced communicating (both present and past tense):

_____   _____

Feelings I mimed:

_____   _____

_____   _____

Feelings I muscled up:

_____   _____

_____   _____

Feelings I switched:

_____   _____

_____   _____

What did I learn about myself today?

_____

_____

🕑 Day 43

Home:

Identified   _____   _____

Communicated _____   _____

Work, school, primary social circle:

Identified   _____   _____

Communicated _____   _____

Out and About:

Identified   _____   _____

Communicated _____   _____

Feelings I wrote out today:

_____   _____

_____   _____

Feelings I practiced communicating (both present and past tense):

_____   _____

Feelings I mimed:

_____   _____

_____   _____

Feelings I muscled up:

_____   _____

_____   _____

Feelings I switched:

_____   _____

_____   _____

What did I learn about myself today?

_____

_____

⏱ Day 44

Home:

Identified   _____   _____

Communicated _____   _____

Work, school, primary social circle:

Identified   _____   _____

Communicated _____   _____

Out and About:

Identified   _____   _____

Communicated _____   _____

Feelings I wrote out today:

_____   _____

_____   _____

Feelings I practiced communicating (both present and past tense):

_____   _____

Feelings I mimed:

_____   _____

_____   _____

Feelings I muscled up:

_____   _____

_____   _____

Feelings I switched:

_____   _____

_____   _____

What did I learn about myself today?

_____

_____

Day 45

Home:

Identified   _____   _____

Communicated _____   _____

Work, school, primary social circle:

Identified   _____   _____

Communicated _____   _____

Out and About:

Identified   _____   _____

Communicated _____   _____

Feelings I wrote out today:

_____   _____

_____   _____

Feelings I practiced communicating (both present and past tense):

_____   _____

Feelings I mimed:

_____   _____

_____   _____

Feelings I muscled up:

_____   _____

_____   _____

Feelings I switched:

_____   _____

_____   _____

What did I learn about myself today?

_____

_____

Day 46

Home:

Identified   _____   _____

Communicated _____   _____

Work, school, primary social circle:

Identified   _____   _____

Communicated _____   _____

Out and About:

Identified   _____   _____

Communicated _____   _____

Feelings I wrote out today:

_____   _____

_____   _____

Feelings I practiced communicating (both present and past tense):

_____   _____

Feelings I mimed:

_____   _____

_____   _____

Feelings I muscled up:

_____   _____

_____   _____

Feelings I switched:

_____   _____

_____   _____

What did I learn about myself today?

_____

_____

🕐 Day 47

Home:

Identified   _____   _____

Communicated _____   _____

Work, school, primary social circle:

Identified   _____   _____

Communicated _____   _____

Out and About:

Identified   _____   _____

Communicated _____   _____

Feelings I wrote out today:

_____   _____

_____   _____

Feelings I practiced communicating (both present and past tense):

_____   _____

Feelings I mimed:

_____   _____

_____   _____

Feelings I muscled up:

_____   _____

_____   _____

Feelings I switched:

_____   _____

_____   _____

What did I learn about myself today?

_____

_____

Day 48

Home:

Identified _____ _____

Communicated _____ _____

Work, school, primary social circle:

Identified _____ _____

Communicated _____ _____

Out and About:

Identified _____ _____

Communicated _____ _____

Feelings I wrote out today:

_____ _____

_____ _____

Feelings I practiced communicating (both present and past tense):

_____ _____

Feelings I mimed:

_____ _____

_____ _____

Feelings I muscled up:

_____   _____

_____   _____

Feelings I switched:

_____   _____

_____   _____

What did I learn about myself today?

_____

_____

🌐 Day 49

Home:

Identified   _____   _____

Communicated _____   _____

Work, school, primary social circle:

Identified   _____   _____

Communicated _____   _____

Out and About:

Identified   _____   _____

Communicated _____   _____

Feelings I wrote out today:

_____   _____

_____   _____

Feelings I practiced communicating (both present and past tense):

_____   _____

Feelings I mimed:

_____   _____

_____   _____

Feelings I muscled up:

_____   _____

_____   _____

Feelings I switched:

_____   _____

_____   _____

What did I learn about myself today?

_____

_____

Day 50

Home:

Identified _____   _____

Communicated _____   _____

Work, school, primary social circle:

Identified _____   _____

Communicated _____   _____

Out and About:

Identified _____   _____

Communicated _____   _____

Feelings I wrote out today:

_____   _____

_____   _____

Feelings I practiced communicating (both present and past tense):

_____   _____

Feelings I mimed:

_____   _____

_____   _____

Feelings I muscled up:

_____   _____

_____   _____

Feelings I switched:

_____   _____

_____   _____

What did I learn about myself today?

_____

_____

Day 51

Home:

Identified   _____   _____

Communicated _____   _____

Work, school, primary social circle:

Identified   _____   _____

Communicated _____   _____

Out and About:

Identified   _____   _____

Communicated _____   _____

Feelings I wrote out today:

_____   _____

_____   _____

Feelings I practiced communicating (both present and past tense):

_____   _____

Feelings I mimed:

_____   _____

_____   _____

Feelings I muscled up:

_____   _____

_____   _____

Feelings I switched:

_____   _____

_____   _____

What did I learn about myself today?

_____

_____

Home:

Identified _____   _____

Communicated _____   _____

Work, school, primary social circle:

Identified _____   _____

Communicated _____   _____

Out and About:

Identified _____   _____

Communicated _____   _____

Feelings I wrote out today:

_____   _____

_____   _____

Feelings I practiced communicating (both present and past tense):

_____   _____

Feelings I mimed:

_____   _____

_____   _____

Feelings I muscled up:

_____   _____

_____   _____

Feelings I switched:

_____   _____

_____   _____

What did I learn about myself today?

_____

_____

🕑 Day 53

Home:

Identified   _____   _____

Communicated _____   _____

Work, school, primary social circle:

Identified   _____   _____

Communicated _____   _____

Out and About:

Identified   _____   _____

Communicated _____   _____

Feelings I wrote out today:

_____   _____

_____   _____

Feelings I practiced communicating (both present and past tense):

_____   _____

Feelings I mimed:

_____   _____

_____   _____

Feelings I muscled up:

_____   _____

_____   _____

Feelings I switched:

_____   _____

_____   _____

What did I learn about myself today?

_____

_____

Day 54

Home:

Identified _____   _____

Communicated _____   _____

Work, school, primary social circle:

Identified _____   _____

Communicated _____   _____

Out and About:

Identified _____   _____

Communicated _____   _____

Feelings I wrote out today:

_____   _____

_____   _____

Feelings I practiced communicating (both present and past tense):

_____   _____

Feelings I mimed:

_____   _____

_____   _____

Feelings I muscled up:

_____   _____

_____   _____

Feelings I switched:

_____   _____

_____   _____

What did I learn about myself today?

_____

_____

Day 55

Home:

Identified   _____   _____

Communicated _____   _____

Work, school, primary social circle:

Identified   _____   _____

Communicated _____   _____

Out and About:

Identified   _____   _____

Communicated _____   _____

Feelings I wrote out today:

_____   _____

_____   _____

Feelings I practiced communicating (both present and past tense):

_____   _____

Feelings I mimed:

_____   _____

_____   _____

Feelings I muscled up:

_____   _____

_____   _____

Feelings I switched:

_____   _____

_____   _____

What did I learn about myself today?

_____

_____

⏱ Day 56

Home:

Identified _____   _____

Communicated _____   _____

Work, school, primary social circle:

Identified _____   _____

Communicated _____   _____

Out and About:

Identified _____   _____

Communicated _____   _____

Feelings I wrote out today:

_____   _____

_____   _____

Feelings I practiced communicating (both present and past tense):

_____   _____

Feelings I mimed:

_____   _____

_____   _____

Feelings I muscled up:

_____   _____

_____   _____

Feelings I switched:

_____   _____

_____   _____

What did I learn about myself today?

_____

_____

Day 57

Home:

Identified   _____   _____

Communicated _____   _____

Work, school, primary social circle:

Identified   _____   _____

Communicated _____   _____

Out and About:

Identified   _____   _____

Communicated _____   _____

Feelings I wrote out today:

_____   _____

_____   _____

Feelings I practiced communicating (both present and past tense):

_____   _____

Feelings I mimed:

_____   _____

_____   _____

Feelings I muscled up:

_____   _____

_____   _____

Feelings I switched:

_____   _____

_____   _____

What did I learn about myself today?

_____

_____

Day 58

Home:

Identified   _____   _____

Communicated _____   _____

Work, school, primary social circle:

Identified   _____   _____

Communicated _____   _____

Out and About:

Identified   _____   _____

Communicated _____   _____

Feelings I wrote out today:

_____   _____

_____   _____

Feelings I practiced communicating (both present and past tense):

_____   _____

Feelings I mimed:

_____   _____

_____   _____

Feelings I muscled up:

_____   _____

_____   _____

Feelings I switched:

_____   _____

_____   _____

What did I learn about myself today?

_____

_____

🕚 Day 59

Home:

Identified   _____   _____

Communicated _____   _____

Work, school, primary social circle:

Identified   _____   _____

Communicated _____   _____

Out and About:

Identified   _____   _____

Communicated _____   _____

Feelings I wrote out today:

_____   _____

_____   _____

Feelings I practiced communicating (both present and past tense):

_____   _____

Feelings I mimed:

_____   _____

_____   _____

Feelings I muscled up:

_____   _____

_____   _____

Feelings I switched:

_____   _____

_____   _____

What did I learn about myself today?

_____

_____

⏱ Day 60

Home:

Identified _____   _____

Communicated _____   _____

Work, school, primary social circle:

Identified _____   _____

Communicated _____   _____

Out and About:

Identified _____   _____

Communicated _____   _____

Feelings I wrote out today:

_____   _____

_____   _____

Feelings I practiced communicating (both present and past tense):

_____   _____

Feelings I mimed:

_____   _____

_____   _____

Feelings I muscled up:

_____   _____

_____   _____

Feelings I switched:

_____   _____

_____   _____

What did I learn about myself today?

_____

_____

You have most likely done more emotional internal work than anyone you know. You should be feeling more connected to yourself, more relaxed with yourself, more authentic, and more in control of your emotions. Your work is a great foundation for the rest of your life as you seek to stay emotionally fit.

I have been communicating two feelings a day with my wife the past twenty-eight years. I know the benefits of emotional fitness for myself, my family, my clients, my coworkers, and my friends. Your work can give you a whole new way of living emotionally fit. Congratulations for taking this journey. I am so proud of you!

APPENDIX

Feelings List

Abandoned	Alive	Authentic	Bossy	Chipper
Abased	Alone	Available	Bothered	Choked-up
Abiding	Alluring	Avenged	Boxed-in	Chosen
Able	Amazed	Avoided	Brainwashed	Circumspect
Abnormal	Amazing	Aware	Bratty	Civil
Abrasive	Ambivalent	Awe	Brave	Claustrophobic
Abrupt	Amused	Awesome	Breathless	Clean
Absent	Analytical	Awestruck	Bristling	Cleansed
Absorbed	Analyzed	Awful	Broken	Clear
Abused	Anchored	Awkward	Broken-up	Clever
Aching	Angry	Babied	Bruised	Close
Acceptable	Anguished	Backward	Bubbly	Closed
Accepted	Animated	Bad	Bugged	Cloudy
Accepting	Animosity	Badgered	Buoyant	Clueless
Accommodating	Annoyed	Baffled	Burdened	Clumsy
Accomplished	Antagonistic	Baited	Burned	Cocky
Accountable	Antisocial	Balanced	Burnt out	Codependent
Accused	Anxiety	Ballistic	Busted	Coerced
Acknowledged	Anxious	Bashful	Bullied	Cold
Active	Apart	Battered	Buried	Collected
Adaptable	Apathy	Beat	Busy	Comatose
Adamant	Apathetic	Beaten	Caged	Combative
Addicted	Apologetic	Beautiful	Calculating	Comfortable
Adequate	Appalled	Befriended	Callous	Comforted
Admirable	Appreciated	Behind	Calm	Commanding
Admiration	Appreciative	Belligerent	Capable	Committed
Admired	Apprehensive	Belittled	Captive	Communicative
Admonished	Approachable	Beloved	Captivated	Compared
Adored	Appropriate	Benevolent	Cared for	Compassionate
Adrift	Approved	Berated	Carefree	Compatible
Adventurous	Argumentative	Bereaved	Careful	Compelled
Affected	Aroused	Betrayed	Careless	Competent
Affection	Arrogant	Bewildered	Caring	Competitive
Affectionate	Articulate	Biased	Caught	Complacent
Afflicted	Artificial	Bitter	Cautious	Complaint
Affirmed	Ashamed	Blamed	Centered	Complete
Afraid	Aspiring	Blaming	Certain	Complicated
Aggravated	Assaulted	Blasted	Challenged	Complimented
Aggressive	Assertive	Bleak	Chaotic	Composed
Agitated	Assisted	Blessed	Chased	Compromised
Agony	Assured	Blind	Charged	Compromising
Agonized	Astonished	Blissful	Charismatic	Compulsive
Agreeable	At ease	Blocked	Charitable	Conceited
Ahead	Attached	Blossoming	Charming	Concerned
Aimless	Attacked	Boastful	Cheap	Condemned
Alarmed	Attentive	Boiling	Cheated	Condescending
Alert	Attracted	Bold	Cheerful	Confident
Alienated	Attractive	Bonded	Childish	Confined
Aloof	Attuned	Bored	Childlike	Confirmed

Conflicted	Cramped	Definite	Diminished	Distrustful
Conforming	Cranky	Deflated	Direct	Disturbed
Confounded	Crass	Degraded	Directionless	Ditched
Confronted	Credible	Dehumanized	Dirty	Divided
Confronting	Crazed	Delayed	Disagreeable	Docile
Confused	Crazy	Delicate	Disappointed	Dogmatic
Congenial	Creative	Delighted	Disapproving	Domestic
Connected	Credible	Delightful	Disarmed	Dominate
Conned	Crippled	Delirious	Disbelieving	Dominated
Conniving	Critical	Delivered	Discarded	Domineering
Conscientious	Criticized	Deluded	Disciplined	Doomed
Consecrated	Cross	Demanding	Discombobulated	Doting
Conservative	Crucified	Demeaned	Disconnected	Doubtful
Considerate	Crude	Democratic	Discounted	Down
Consistent	Cruel	Demolished	Discouraged	Downhearted
Consoled	Crummy	Demoralized	Discreet	Drained
Consoling	Crushed	Demoted	Discredited	Dramatic
Constrained	Cuddled	Demotivated	Discriminating	Dread
Constricted	Cuddly	Denigrated	Disempowered	Dreadful
Constructive	Culpable	Dense	Disenchanted	Dreamy
Consulted	Cultured	Dependable	Disengaged	Driven
Consumed	Cunning	Dependent	Disgraced	Dull
Contagious	Curious	Depleted	Disgusted	Dumb
Contained	Cursed	Depreciated	Disheartened	Dutiful
Contemplative	Cut	Depressed	Disheveled	Dysfunctional
Contempt	Cute	Deprived	Dishonest	Eager
Content	Cynical	Deserted	Dishonorable	Earnest
Contrary	Damaged	Deserving	Disillusioned	Earthly
Contributing	Damned	Desirable	Disinterested	Easy going
Contrite	Dangerous	Desire	Dismayed	Eccentric
Controlled	Daring	Desired	Dismissed	Ecstatic
Controlling	Dark	Despair	Dismissive	Edgy
Conventional	Dazed	Desperate	Displeased	Edified
Convicted	Dead	Despicable	Disobedient	Educated
Convinced	Debased	Despised	Disobeyed	Effective
Convincing	Deceitful	Despondent	Disorderly	Egoistical
Cool	Deceived	Destroyed	Disorganized	Elated
Cooperative	Decent	Detailed	Disoriented	Eloquent
Copied	Deceptive	Destroyed	Dispassionate	Elusive
Correct	Decisive	Detached	Dispirited	Emancipated
Courageous	Dedicated	Devalued	Displeased	Embarrassed
Courteous	Deep	Devastated	Disregarded	Emotional
Coveted	Defeated	Devious	Disrespected	Encouraged
Cowardly	Defective	Devoted	Disruptive	Emotionless
Coy	Defenseless	Devout	Dissatisfied	Empathetic
Cozy	Defensive	Different	Distant	Empowered
Crabby	Defiant	Difficult	Distracted	Empty
Crashed	Deficient	Dignified	Distressed	Enabled
Crafty	Defiled	Diligent	Distrusted	Enchanted

Endeared	Faded	Forsaken	Gregarious	Horrible
Endearing	Faith	Fortified	Grief	Horrified
Engrossed	Faithful	Fortunate	Grieved	Hostile
Enjoyment	Fake	Fragile	Grim	Hounded
Enlightened	Fallible	Fragmented	Grimy	Humane
Enmeshed	Famished	Frantic	Grouchy	Humble
Enraged	Fanatical	Frazzled	Grounded	Humbled
Enraptured	Fantastic	Free	Grumpy	Humiliated
Enriched	Fascinated	Friendly	Guarded	Humored
Enslaved	Fascinating	Frightened	Guided	Hurried
Enterprising	Fatalistic	Frisky	Guilty	Hustled
Entertained	Fatigued	Frivolous	Gutsy	Hurt
Entertaining	Favored	Frolicsome	Haggled	Hyper
Enticed	Fear	Frugal	Hammered	Hysterical
Enthralled	Fearful	Fruitful	Happy	Idealistic
Enthusiastic	Fearless	Frustrated	Harassed	Idiotic
Entitled	Feeble	Fulfilled	Hard	Idle
Entrepreneurial	Feisty	Full	Hardened	Ignorant
Entrusted	Ferocious	Fuming	Hardy	Ignored
Envious	Fervent	Fun	Harmed	Ill
Equal	Festive	Functional	Harmless	Imaginative
Equipped	Fickle	Funky	Harness	Imbalanced
Erratic	Fidgety	Funloving	Harried	Immature
Established	Fierce	Funny	Hassled	Immune
Esteemed	Fiery	Furious	Hasty	Impaired
Estranged	Finicky	Fussy	Hate	Impartial
Evaded	Firm	Gabby	Haughty	Impatient
Evasive	Fit	Generous	Healthy	Imperfect
Exasperated	Fixated	Gentle	Heard	Impermeable
Exasperation	Flabbergasted	Genuine	Heartbroken	Impervious
Excellent	Flamboyant	Giddy	Hearty	Important
Excessive	Flashy	Gifted	Heartless	Imposed-upon
Excited	Flawed	Giving	Heavy	Imposing
Exempt	Flexible	Glad	Heckled	Impotent
Exhilarated	Floored	Gloomy	Helped	Impoverished
Expansive	Flourishing	Glorious	Helpful	Impractical
Expectant	Flustered	Glowing	Helpless	Impressed
Experienced	Focused	Gluttonous	Heroic	Impulsive
Experimental	Foggy	Good-looking	Hesitant	In control
Exploitative	Followed	Good-natured	Hindered	Inaccessible
Exploited	Fond	Goofy	Hip	Inactive
Explosive	Foolhardy	Graceful	High	Inadequate
Exposed	Foolish	Gracious	Hollow	Inappropriate
Expressive	Forced	Grand	Homesick	Incapable
Extraordinary	Forceful	Grandiose	Honest	Incapacitated
Extravagant	Forgetful	Grateful	Honorable	Incensed
Extreme	Forgiven	Gratified	Honored	Incoherent
Exuberant	Forgiving	Great	Hopeful	Incommunicative
Fabulous	Forgotten	Greedy	Hopeless	Incompatible

Incompetent	Interesting	Lamenting	Maniacal	Modest
Incomplete	Interrupted	Languishing	Manic	Monitored
Incongruent	Intimate	Late	Manipulated	Moody
Inconsiderate	Intimidated	Lazy	Manipulative	Mopey
Inconsistent	Intimidating	Led astray	Manly	Moral
Inconsolable	Intrigued	Leaned on	Marginalized	Morbid
Inconvenienced	Intolerant	Leery	Marvelous	Morose
Incredible	Introspective	Left out	Masterful	Mortified
Incredulous	Introverted	Legitimate	Materialistic	Mothered
Indebted	Intuitive	Let down	Maternal	Motivated
Indecisive	Invalidated	Lethargic	Mature	Mournful
Independent	Invalidating	Liberal	Maudlin	Mundane
Indifferent	Inventive	Liberated	Meager	Mushy
Indignant	Invigorated	Lifeless	Mean	Musical
Indirect	Invisible	Likeable	Medicated	Muzzled
Indoctrinated	Invited	Light-hearted	Mediocre	Mystified
Indulgent	Inviting	Limited	Meditative	Nagged
Industrious	Involved	Limp	Meek	Nailed
Ineffective	Irate	Listened to	Melancholy	Naïve
Inefficient	Irked	Listless	Melancholic	Naked
Inexperienced	Irrational	Little	Mellow	Narcissistic
Infantile	Irrelevant	Lively	Menacing	Narrow-minded
Infatuated	Irresistible	Livid	Mended	Nasty
Infected	Irresponsible	Loathing	Merciful	Naughty
Inferior	Irreverent	Logical	Merry	Nauseated
Inflated	Irritable	Lonely	Mesmerized	Neat
Inflexible	Irritated	Longing	Messy	Needed
Influenced	Isolated	Loose	Methodical	Needled
Influential	Jaded	Lost	Meticulous	Needy
Informed	Jealous	Loud	Miffed	Negated
Infuriated	Jeopardized	Lousy	Militant	Neglected
Ingenious	Jittery	Lovable	Mindful	Negligent
Inhibited	Jovial	Love	Mindless	Neighborly
Injured	Joyous	Loved	Minimized	Nervous
Innocent	Jubilant	Loving	Mischievous	Nervy
Innovative	Judged	Low	Miserable	Neurotic
Insecure	Judgmental	Loyal	Miserly	Neutral
Insensitive	Judicious	Lucky	Misguided	Nice
Insightful	Jumpy	Lured	Misled	Nit-picky
Insignificant	Keen	Luring	Misrepresented	Noble
Insincere	Kind	Lust	Mistaken	Nonchalant
Inspired	Knotted up	Lustful	Mistreated	Noncommittal
Instinctive	Knowledgeable	Mad	Mistrustful	Nonconforming
Insulated	Known	Magnificent	Misunderstood	Nonexistent
Intelligent	Labeled	Malaise	Mixed-up	Normal
Intense	Lackadaisical	Malicious	Mobile	Nostalgic
Intent	Lacking	Maligned	Mobilized	Nosy
Intentional	Laid-back	Manageable	Mocked	Noticed
Interested	Lame	Managed	Mocking	Nourished

Nudged
Nullified
Numb
Nursed
Nurtured
Nurturing
Nuts
Obedient
Objectified
Obligated
Obliging
Oblivious
Obnoxious
Obscene
Obscured
Observant
Observed
Obsessed
Obsolete
Obstinate
Obstructed
Offended
Offensive
Old
Old-fashioned
On
Open
Open-minded
Opinionated
Opportunistic
Oppositional
Oppressed
Optimistic
Opulent
Orderly
Organized
Ornery
Orphaned
Ostentatious
Ostracized
Ousted
Out of balance
Out of control
Out of it
Out of place
Out of touch
Outdated
Outdone
Outgoing

Outlandish
Outnumbered
Outraged
Outrageous
Outranked
Outspoken
Over-prepared
Over-protected
Overcome
Overbearing
Overjoyed
Overlooked
Overpowered
Overweight
Overwhelmed
Overworked
Overzealous
Pacified
Pain
Pampered
Panic
Panicked
Paralyzed
Pardoned
Paranoid
Passed up
Passionate
Passive
Paternal
Pathetic
Patient
Patronized
Peaceful
Peaked
Peculiar
Peeved
Penetrated
Pensive
Peppy
Perceptive
Perfectionistic
Peripheral
Perky
Permeable
Perplexed
Persecuted
Persistent
Persuasive
Pertinent

Perturbed
Pessimistic
Pestered
Petered-out
Petrified
Petty
Philanthropic
Phony
Picked apart
Picked on
Pierced
Pining
Pissed
Pitied
Pity
Placid
Plagued
Plain
Planless
Playful
Pleading
Pleasant
Pleased
Pleasure
Plundered
Poisoned
Polite
Polluted
Pompous
Pooped
Popular
Positive
Possessive
Potent
Pouty
Powerful
Powerless
Practical
Praised
Pragmatic
Preached to
Precious
Precocious
Preoccupied
Prepared
Present
Pressed
Pressured
Prestigious

Presumptuous
Pretentious
Pretty
Pride
Primal
Primitive
Private
Privileged
Proactive
Probed
Productive
Professional
Progressing
Promiscuous
Promoted
Proper
Prophetic
Prosecuted
Prosperous
Protected
Protective
Proud
Provocative
Provoked
Psyched
Pulled
Pulled apart
Pulverized
Pumped
Punctual
Punched
Punished
Puny
Pure
Purged
Purposeful
Pursued
Pushed
Pushy
Put down
Puzzled
Qualified
Quarrelsome
Queasy
Questioned
Quick
Quiet
Radiant
Radical

Rage
Rageful
Raging
Railroaded
Raped
Rational
Rattled
Rauchy
Ravenous
Ravished
Ravishing
Raw
Re-energized
Re-enforced
Reachable
Reactionary
Reactive
Ready
Real
Realistic
Reamed out
Reasonable
Reassured
Rebellious
Reborn
Rebounding
Rebuked
Receptive
Recharged
Reckless
Reclusive
Recognized
Reconciled
Recuperated
Recovered
Recruited
Redeemed
Reduced
Refreshed
Refined
Reflective
Refueled
Regressive
Regret
Regretful
Rejected
Rejecting
Rejuvenated
Relaxed

Released	Righteous	Self-acceptance	Silent	Spacey
Relentless	Rigid	Self-assured	Silly	Spared
Reliable	Rigorous	Self-centered	Simple	Spastic
Relieved	Riled	Self-confident	Sincere	Special
Religious	Ripped off	Self-conscious	Sinful	Speechless
Reluctant	Riveted	Self-destructive	Singled-out	Spellbound
Remarkable	Robbed	Self-disciplined	Sinking	Spent
Remembered	Robotic	Self-forgiving	Skeptical	Spineless
Remorse	Robust	Self-love	Skilled	Spirited
Removed	Romantic	Self-pitying	Skillful	Spiteful
Renewed	Rotten	Self-righteous	Skipped	Splendid
Repelled	Rough	Self-sacrificing	Slack	Spoiled
Repentant	Rowdy	Self-serving	Slain	Spontaneous
Replaced	Rude	Selfish	Slandered	Spooked
Replenished	Ruined	Selfless	Slaughtered	Spry
Reprimanded	Run down	Senile	Sleepy	Spunky
Reproached	Rushed	Sensational	Slighted	Squeamish
Repulsed	Ruthless	Sensible	Sloppy	Squelched
Repulsive	Sabotaged	Sensitive	Slothful	Stabbed
Rescued	Sacrificial	Sensual	Slow	Stable
Resentful	Sad	Sensuous	Sluggish	Stained
Reserved	Safe	Sentenced	Sly	Startled
Resigned	Sane	Sentimental	Small	Starved
Resilient	Sarcastic	Separated	Smart	Stereotyped
Resistant	Sassy	Serene	Smitten	Stern
Resolute	Satiated	Serious	Smooth	Stiff
Resolved	Satisfied	Set up	Smothered	Stifled
Resourceful	Saturated	Settled	Smug	Stigmatized
Respected	Saved	Sexy	Snarky	Still
Respectful	Savvy	Shaken	Sneaky	Stingy
Responsible	Scapegoated	Shaky	Snobby	Stimulated
Responsive	Scared	Shallow	Snoopy	Stirred
Repressed	Scarred	Shamed	Snowed	Stoic
Rested	Scheming	Sharp	Snubed	Stopped
Restless	Scintillated	Shattered	Soaring	Strained
Restrained	Scolded	Sheepish	Social	Stranded
Restricted	Scorned	Sheltered	Soft	Strange
Retaliatory	Screwed	Shielded	Sold-out	Strangled
Revealed	Scrutinized	Shocked	Solemn	Strengthened
Revengeful	Searching	Shortchanged	Solid	Stressed
Reverent	Secure	Shot down	Solitary	Stressed out
Revitalized	Sedate	Shredded	Somber	Stretched
Revived	Sedentary	Shrewd	Soothed	Stricken
Revolved	Seduced	Shunned	Sophisticated	Strict
Rewarded	Seductive	Shy	Sore	Strong
Rich	Seeking	Sick	Sorry	Stubborn
Ridiculed	Seething	Sickened	Sorrowful	Stuck
Ridiculous	Selected	Significant	Sound	Studious
Right	Self-absorbed	Silenced	Sour	Stumped

Stunned	Tender	Unblocked	Vibrant	Withdrawn
Stunning	Tense	Unburdened	Victorious	Wobbly
Stunted	Tentative	Uncaged	Vigilant	Wonderful
Stupefied	Terrific	Uncertain	Vigorous	Wondering
Stupendous	Terrified	Unchained	Vilified	Wordy
Stupid	Tested	Unchosen	Vindictive	Woeful
Stylish	Testy	Unclear	Violated	Worn
Suave	Thoughtful	Uncomfortable	Violent	Worn out
Subdued	Threatened	Undercontrol	Virile	Worried
Subjugated	Thrifty	Understanding	Visited	Worshipful
Submissive	Thrilled	Understood	Vital	Worshiping
Subordinate	Thrown	Undesirable	Vocal	Worth
Subservient	Ticked	Unequal	Void	Worthless
Successful	Tickled	Unfriendly	Volatile	Worthy
Suffocated	Tight	Ungrateful	Voluptuous	Wowed
Sulking	Timid	Unguided	Vulnerable	Wrathful
Sullen	Tiny	Unhappy	Wacky	Wrecked
Super	Tired	Unified	Waffling	Wrong
Superficial	Tolerant	Unimpressed	Walled up	Wronged
Superior	Tormented	Unique	Walled off	Yearning
Superstitious	Torn	Unkept	Waning	Yielding
Supported	Tortured	Unkind	Wanting	Yoked
Supportive	Touched	Unliked	Warm	Yucky
Suppressed	Tranquil	Unraveled	Warped	Zany
Sure	Trapped	Unreasonable	Warned	Zealous
Surprised	Tremendous	Unsafe	Wary	Zestful
Surreal	Tricked	Unsettled	Washed	Zippy
Surrendered	Tricky	Unstable	Washed up	
Susceptible	Trivial	Upset	Wasted	
Suspicious	Troubled	Uptight	Watched	
Swamped	True	Unwanted	Watchful	
Sweet	Trusted	Unworthy	Wayward	
Swindled	Trustful	Unwound	Weak	
Sympathy	Trusting	Uprooted	Wealthy	
Tacky	Truthful	Used	Weary	
Tactful	Tuff	Useful	Weepy	
Tainted	Turbulent	Useless	Well	
Talkative	Tutored	Vacant	Whacked	
Tall	Tweaked	Vague	Whining	
Tame	Twisted	Vain	Whipped	
Targeted	Ugly	Valiant	Whole	
Tarnished	Unacceptable	Validated	Wicked	
Taunt	Unable	Valuable	Wild	
Taxed	Unafraid	Valued	Willful	
Teachable	Unamused	Vengeful	Willing	
Tearful	Unapproachable	Venting	Wimpy	
Teary	Unaware	Vetoed	Wiped out	
Teased	Unbelieving	Vexed	Wise	
Tempted	Unbending	Viable	Wishful	

INTIMACY ANOREXIA

This hidden addiction is destroying so many marriages today. In your hands is the first antidote for someone with intimacy anorexia to turn the pages on this addiction process. Excerpts from intimacy anorexics and their spouses help this book become clinically helpful and personal in its impact to communicate hope and healing for the intimacy anorexic and the marriage.

BOOK: $22.95
DVD: $69.95

INTIMACY ANOREXIA: THE WORKBOOK

This is like therapy in a box. Inside is 100 exercises that have already been proven helpful in treating intimacy anorexia.

WORKBOOK: $39.95

INTIMACY ANOREXIA: THE STEPS

This is the only twelve step workbook just for intimacy anorexia. Each step gives you progress in your healing from intimacy anorexia.

STEP BOOK: $14.95

MARRIED & ALONE

This is for the spouse of an intimacy anorexic. You feel disconnected, untouched and often unloved. You are not crazy and Dr. Weiss will help you to start a journey of recovery from living with a spouse with intimacy anorexia.

BOOK: $14.95
DVD: $49.95

MARRIED & ALONE: HEALING EXERCISES FOR SPOUSES

This is the first workbook to offer practical suggestions and techniques to better navigate through recovery from your spouse's Intimacy Anorexia.

WORKBOOK: $39.95

MARRIED & ALONE: THE TWELVE STEP GUIDE

This Twelve Step guide will help the spouse of an intimacy anorexic work through the Twelve Steps that many others have found to be helpful in their recovery.

STEP BOOK: $14.95

SIN OF WITHHOLDING

This DVD is the first to address the Biblical foundation of the sin of withholding in believers' hearts. The practical application in marriage addressing Intimacy Anorexia is also interwoven in this revelational teaching on the Sin of Withholding. Once a believer is free of this sin, their walk with the Lord and their fruit towards others can increase expediently.

DVD SET: $49.95

PAIN FOR LOVE

Pain For Love describes in detail one of the most insidious strategies of an intimacy anorexic with their spouse. This dynamic is experienced by many who are married to an intimacy anorexic. This paradigm can empower the spouse and help them stop participating in a pain for love dynamic in their marriage.

DVD: $29.95

NARCISSISM SEX ADDICTION AND INTIMACY ANOREXIA

The profound information that you will learn in this DVD will help you fairly evaluate your specific situation for narcissism, which will help you develop a treatment plan to address the issue you are dealing with at its core.

DVD: $29.95

MEN'S RECOVERY

THE **FINAL FREEDOM**

DOUGLAS WEISS, PH.D.

This book gives more current information than many professional counselors have today. In addition to informing sex addicts and their partners about sex addiction, it gives hope for recovery. The information provided in this book would cost hundreds of dollars in counseling hours to receive. Many have attested to successful recovery from this information alone.

BOOK: $22.95
CD: $35.00

101 FREEDOM EXERCISES

This is the best single resource for the Christian who desires to know what they need to do to get and stay free from sexual addiction. This book contains 101 exercises that have been proven to work.   WORKBOOK: $39.95

STEPS TO FREEDOM

This is a Christian approach to the Twelve Steps. This book will guide you through the 12 Steps of recovery that have been helpful for many addicted people. This book is specifically written for the person desiring recovery from sexual addiction.

STEP BOOK: $14.95

HELPING HER HEAL

The *Helping Her Heal* DVD is for the man who has disclosed his sexual addiction to his partner or spouse. This DVD offers practical tools for hearing her pain, navigating her grief and losses, discovering her expectations of you and the boundaries she may need to heal.

DVD: $69.95

MARRIED AFTER ADDICTION

Addiction can have devastating effects on even good marriages. In this DVD you are intelligently guided through the journey you will experience if addiction is part of your marriage story. You will learn important information about the early and later stages of recovery for your marriage.

DVD: $29.95

DISCLOSURE

Disclosure is one of the most important topics in sexual addiction recovery. In this DVD, Dr. Weiss discusses the various types of disclosure. Each type of disclosure is for a specific purpose or person. This DVD can expedite the understanding of each of the significant processes of disclosure for the addict, the spouse and the marriage.

DVD: $39.95

SEXUAL TEMPLATES

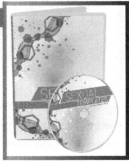

Each of us has a sexual template – a developed pattern in the brain of what we find sexually arousing. Sexual Templates are formed by unique experiences as a person matures. But, how do you change a sexual template if it has negatively impacted your life?

DVD: $29.95

SEX AFTER RECOVERY

If sex addiction, infidelity, or intimacy anorexia have ever been present in your marriage, you and your spouse's sexuality can be impacted both significantly and uniquely. Sex is an important aspect of any marriage. With several decades of experience in the fields of sex addiction, partner betrayal trauma, and intimacy anorexia.

DVD: $59.95

HEALING HER HEART AFTER RELAPSE

This DVD is way more than, "He relapses, he does a consequence and moves on." The addict is given real tools to address the emotional damage and repair of her heart as a result of a relapse. Every couple in recovery would do well to have these tools before a potential relapse.

DVD: $29.95

WOMEN'S RECOVERY

Partners: Healing From His Addiction book is the latest in research of the affects on a woman who has lived with a sexual addict. The riveting statistics combined with personal stories of recovery make this a must read book for any woman in a relationship with a sex addict. This book gives you hope and a beginning plan for personal recovery.

BOOK: $14.95

PARTNER'S RECOVERY GUIDE

This is like therapy in a box for women who want to walk through the residual effects of being in a relationship with a sex addict.

WORKBOOK: $39.95

BEYOND LOVE

This is an interactive workbook that allows the partners of sex addicts to gain insight and strength through working the Twelve Steps.

STEP BOOK: $14.95

HE NEEDS TO CHANGE, DR. WEISS

He Needs To Change, Dr. Weiss DVD addresses the pain, trauma, and betrayal women experience because of their partner's sex addiction, betrayal, and/or intimacy anorexia.In this DVD, Dr. Weiss addresses the issue of change that he has explained to thousands of women in his office.

DVD: $29.95

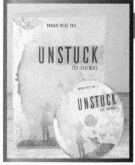

UNSTUCK FOR PARTNERS

The *Unstuck* DVD is for every woman who has experienced the pain of their partner's sex addiction or intimacy anorexia and feels stuck, confused, frustrated and unable to move on. You didn't sign up for this and honestly, you don't get it! This DVD helps you "get it" so you can process the painful reality you are in and start to live again.

DVD: $29.95

PARTNER BETRAYAL TRAUMA

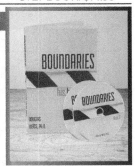

Partner Betrayal Trauma is real. Your pain and experience of betrayal has impacted all of your being and all of your relationships.

The book, DVD set, Workbook and Step guide were designed to help guide you thoughtfully through your own personal healing from the effects of being betrayed by your spouse or significant other. The pain and trauma of being betrayed, especially sexual betrayal, by a spouse or significant other is multidimensional and multifaceted. Your pain and trauma are real and these resources will help you in your journey of recovery from Partner Betrayal Trauma.

BOOK: $22.95   DVD: $65.95   WORKBOOK: $39.95   STEPBOOK: $14.95

BOUNDARIES

Boundaries are a healthy, normal, and necessary part of the recovery process for sex addicts, intimacy anorexics, and their spouses. In this DVD set, Dr. Doug Weiss provides an answer to the clarion call on boundaries by educating and guiding you through this process.   DVD: $49.95

MOVING FORWARD

Dealing with the aftermath of a divorce can feel like emotional roller coaster ride. After years or decades of being married, it does take time to get out of the routine of being married and start living as a single woman again. Though being married to a sex addict or intimacy anorexic may have caused you pain, it does not need to control or define who you are or your future.   DVD: $29.95

MARRIAGE RESOURCES

LOVER SPOUSE

Lover Spouse helps you understand marriage from a Christ-centered perspective. Christian Marriages were designed to be different, passionate, fulfilling, and long-lasting.   BOOK: $13.95

UPGRADE YOUR SEX LIFE

Upgrade Your Sex Life actually teaches you own unique sexual expression that you and your partner are pre-wired to enjoy.
BOOK: $16.95 DVD:29.95

SERVANT MARRIAGE

Servant Marriage book is a Revelation on God's Masterpiece of marriage. In these pages, you will walk with God as He creates the man, the woman and his masterpiece called marriage.
BOOK: $13.95

MARRIAGE MONDAYS

This is an eight week marriage training that actually gives you the skills to have a healthy and more vibrant marriage.
          BOOK: $16.95

INTIMACY

This 100 Day guide can transform couples from any level of intimacy to a lifestyle of satiation with their spouse.   BOOK: $11.95

MIRACLE OF MARRIAGE

God made your marriage to be an amazing and unique miracle. Dr. Weiss walks you through the creation and maintenance of your marriage. You will be exposed to a practical insights that can help make your marriage into God's original design.
DVD: $12.95

OTHER RESOURCES

WORTHY: EXERCISES & STEP BOOK

The *Worthy* Workbook and DVD, is designed for a 12 week study. Here is a path that anyone can take to get and stay worthy. Follow this path, and you too will make the journey from worthless to worthy just as others have.

DVD: $29.95
BOOK: $29.95

EMOTIONAL FITNESS

Everyone has an unlimited number of emotions, but few have been trained to identify, choose, communicate, and master them. More than a guide for gaining emotional fitness and mastery, in these pages you will find a pathway to a much more fulfilling life.

BOOK: $16.95

LETTERS TO MY DAUGHTER

A gift for your daugher as she enters college. *Letters to my Daughter* includes my daily letters to my daughter during her first year of college.

BOOK: $14.95

BORN FOR WAR

Born for War teaches practical tools to defeat these sexual landmines and offers scriptural truths that empower young men to desire successfulness in the war thrust upon them.

DVD: $29.95

PRINCES TAKE LONGER THAN FROGS

This 2 hour DVD helps single women ages 15-30, to successfully navigate through the season of dating.

DVD: $29.95

SUCCESSFULLY SINGLE

This 2 Disc DVD Series is definitely nothing you have heard before. Dr. Weiss charts new territory as to the why for sexual purity.

DVD: $29.95

SERIES FOR MEN

CLEAN

BOOK: $16.95
DVD: $29.95
JOURNAL: $16.95

Every Christian man is born into a sexual war. The enemy attacks the young, hoping to scar them permanently and leave them ruined. Your past is not enough to keep you from the enduringly clean life you want and deserve. This series can be used individually or in a small group setting.

LUST FREE LIVING

Every man can fight for and obtain a lust free lifestyle. Once you know how to stop lust, you will realize how weak lust really can be. God gace you the power to protect those you love from the ravages of lust for the rest of your life! It's time to take it back!

BOOK: $13.95
DVD: $23.95

MEN MAKE MEN

Dr. Weiss takes the listeners by the hand and step-by-step walks through the creative process God used to make every man into a man of God. This practical teaching on DVD combined with the Men Make Guidebook can revitalize the men in any home or local church.

DVD: $29.95
GUIDEBOOK: $11.95

NEW PRODUCTS

A·A·S·A·T

American Association for Sex Addiction Therapy

SEX ADDICTION TRAINING SET

Both men and women are seeking to counsel more than ever for sexually addictive behaviors. You can be prepared! Forty-seven hours of topics related to sexual addiction treatment are covered in this training including:
- The Six Types of Sex Addicts
- Neurological Understanding
- Sex and Recovery
- Relapse Strategies

TRAINING SET: $1195

PARTNER'S RECOVERY TRAINING SET

With this AASAT training, you will gain proven clinical insight into treating the issues facing partners. You can be prepared! Thirty-nine hours of topics related to partners treatment are covered in this training, including:
- Partner Model
- Partner Grief
- Anger
- Boundaries

TRAINING SET: $995

INTIMACY ANOREXIA TRAINING SET

This growing issue of Intimacy Anorexia will need your competent help in your community. Now, you can be prepared to identify it and treat it. In this training you'll cover topics like:
- Identifying Intimacy Anorexia
- Causes of Intimacy Anorexia
- Treatment Plan
- Relapse Strategies

TRAINING SET: $995

FOR MORE INFORMATION VISIST WWW.AASAT.ORG OR CALL 719.330.2425

cereset™

Heart to Heart Counseling Center has recently acquired Cereset, the most technologically advanced neuromodulation software available. It has received 13 peer review publications, and 9 Institutional Review Boards (IRB) clinically approved trials including the US Military.

By rebalancing and recalibrating the brain, it has helped anxiety, PTSD, trauma, sleeplessness, addiction, low mood and energy, TBI, stress management and neuroplasticity in many of my clients. Most spouses at Heart to Heart Counseling Center have many of the PTSD symptoms from betrayal. More than 80% of those with addiction have unresolved traumas as part of their story.

The brain is your central command center. When your brain is out of balance, or stuck, you don't feel right and it's impossible to function at your highest level. Cereset is a proven technology that's non-invasive and highly effective. Cereset can help your brain free itself, enabling you to achieve higher levels of well-being and balance throughout your life.

Here's what clients had to say about Cereset Garden of the Gods after their sessions:

> *"I'm waking up earlier and feeling more rested and alert. Anxiety is lessened. PTSD symptoms alleviated. Lessened food cravings and quantity of food reduced. Arthritis symptoms improved. I feel more relaxed, less angry and reactive."*

The cost for five sessions (one per day) is $1,500.

For more information call us at 719-278-3708

Made in the USA
Coppell, TX
16 March 2024